To the Mountain and Back

To the Mountain and Back
The Mysteries of Guatemalan Highland Family Life

Jody Glittenberg

WAVELAND
PRESS, INC.

Prospect Heights, Illinois

For information about this book, write or call:

Waveland Press, Inc.
P.O. Box 400
Prospect Heights, Illinois 60070
(847) 634-0081

Photographs appearing on pages 8, 21, 24, 33, 37, 52, 57, 103, 138, and 143 courtesy of Ulli Steltzer. Used with permission.

Printed in the United States of America

7   6   5   4   3

Contents

Acknowledgments

The endeavor of writing a book owes much to many. I wish to thank first, my parents, Fred and Ella Kropp. My mother, foreign-born, in Denmark, taught me early in life to respect other cultures by getting to know them; her kindness was cross-cultural. My father, German-speaking, and a social reformer before we knew the term, taught me to put love into action. My brothers and sisters, Daryl, Ardis, Allen, Jim, and Janice (and their spouses), gave me, throughout my unconventional life, the security of an unconditional love, faith in humanity, and role models for living life fully and without fear. My children, Paul and Janis, gave me reasons for living, and they are still my well of creativity. You shared most of my discoveries and adventures in the field; this story is about us and how we grew and survived as outsiders with insider strengths. I owe much to my former husband, Don. You were a faithful, loving husband and father during my many absences; I sincerely respect you and thank you.

My longtime friend and mentor, Madeleine Leininger, you gave me encouragement to fly high and sometimes dangerously in pursuit of truth. I still owe much to my dissertation advisor, Waldemar Smith; I admire him for his honesty and integrity.

My Guatemalan friend and mentor, Dr. Eugénio Schieber, you are remembered with deepest respect, for you taught me the beauty of the land you love; you shared your *chispa de la vida* with me and made the fieldwork come to life. Dr. Carroll Behrhorst—Doc— gave me my first comprehension of what primary health care and health care reform are all about; it was an essential beginning.

Thanks must go to the program managers of the National Science Foundation, who carved out a program of financial support for dissertations, which although small in actual dollars, made the difference in the actual depth of my findings. I hope my success has helped inform legislators of the importance of supporting budding scientists as a public trust.

Certainly neither last, nor least, I acknowledge the people of Guatemala—and especially of Zaragoza and Patzún—who accepted the *gringa* and her family, shared their life stories, and opened their hearts during times of troubles. There are so many specific *guatemaltecos* who taught me so much. I will name but a few: Eugénio, Margarita, Julio Cesar, Jerry, María, Aña, Sandra, Juan, Silvia; and also: Elmer, Doc, and Jenny, who were so influential. Several have died, some at the hands of assassins; I miss you.

And, not ever to be forgotten, Tom Curtin, anthropology editor at Waveland Press, who five years ago began asking me to write my story. Thanks, Tom, for your encouragement, your persistent nudging, and your outstanding editorship.

Participants

Colorado Family

Don, husband
Paul, son
Janis, daughter
Author's names: JoAnn, Jody, Juanita (used differently in various
　　settings)

In Chimaltenango, Behrhorst Hospital and Clinic

Baby Rosa, a significant infant
Dr. Carroll Behrhorst, medical missionary from Kansas, 1959–1990
Edith Sherwood, British midwife, medical assistant, and director
　　of under-five clinics and literacy program
John McCory, Peace Corps volunteer, medical assistant, at the
　　hospital/clinic and outlying clinics
Margarita, Mayan head nurse in the hospital
Mike, Peace Corps volunteer, assistant in the 1971 surgery
Sally, American missionary nurse from Denver

In Xajáxac

El brujo (witch doctor), one of seventy-five in the village
Magdelena Katok, Mayan nurse in charge of the village clinic

In Zaragoza: The Ladino Town

Andradé family, a modernizing family: Carmen, Humberto, and
　　three children, live with Carmen's widowed mother
Anna López, widow, interviewer for the fertility questionnaires
Don Marquez, host for the cofradia celebration
Hermana Marta, one of six Guatemalan Catholic nuns living in a
　　convent in the cathedral
Hernández family, poorest-of-the-poor:
　　Tina (mother) and Jorge (father), Juan (10), Franco (8), Juanita
　　(5), Dahlia (4), Miguel (6 mos.)
Isabela, an aging neighbor, first wife, with ten adult children:

ix

Alberto, a farmer and eldest son; Juanita, her youngest, and Marta, her modernizing daughters living at home
Miguel, her wandering husband
Jorge Martínez, school teacher
Author's fictive Marquez family:
Silvia (mother) and Pablo (father), Victoria (25-year-old daughter), Antonia (22-year-old daughter), Juan (Victoria's novio, a traveling businessman), Mario (Antonia's novio, a local carpenter)
Mayor and his wife
Olympia Lucas, lives in Los Angeles, queen of the Corpus Christi Fiesta
Padre Pius, town's Italian Catholic priest
Roberto, a handsome *muy hombre* (local term), would-be suitor

In Patzún: The Indian Town

Caj family, poorest-of-the-poor:
Concepción (mother) and Leonardo (father), Lucio (8), Felicia (6), Hermando (2)
Chief public health officer, a barrier to literacy
Felipa Noj, Cakchiquel/Spanish interviewer for the fertility questionnaires
Hortensia, president of the Women's Club of Patzún, her husband, Ernesto, and their three children
Author's fictive Maczul family:
Mother, Father, Maria and Gloria (unmarried daughters), Alberto (the eldest Maczul son) and his wife and three children, the second-eldest son and his wife and five children, and the eldest daughter and her husband and three children
Maria, author's assistant interviewer, Cakchiquel/Spanish speaker
Mayor and town clerk
Padre Sergio, town's Spanish Catholic priest
Christiana and Sonia, American nuns at the Colégio San Bernardino
Strong older woman, berater of the attacking mob

Others

Dr. Eugénio Schieber, a friend whose home is near Lake Atitlán
Gary Elbow, cultural geographer, doctoral student from the University of Texas
Maximón, a folk saint
Muñeca, the author's pet dog
Two American passers-by, Ed and Pete

Chapter 1

Introduction

Our work is to show we have been breathed upon . . . to sing it out, to live out in the topside world what we have received through our sudden knowings from story, from body, from dreams and journeys of all sorts.
—Clarissa Pinkola Estés, *Women Who Run with the Wolves*, 1992

Early American anthropologists such as Ruth Benedict, Margaret Mead, Clyde Kluckhohn and others studied whole cultures as patterns, configurations, and—in some ways—as riddles. Anthropologists have continued to study societies as systems of beliefs, values, rules, and practices that fit into patterns. To explain such patterns, we must assume that life is not just random, but rather that there are reasons why people value some things over others and why they believe and behave as they do.

Marvin Harris, a contemporary anthropologist, in 1975 published a best-selling book, *Cows, Pigs, Wars, and Witches: The Riddles of Culture*. In this book, Harris explains the different patterns of culture, such as not eating the sacred cow among the Hindus, as riddles that have down-to-earth, practical explanations. As Harris explains, to understand the riddle, one must examine the whole society in order to be aware of how the parts fit together into a pattern, like a puzzle. The backbone of an anthropologist's work is unraveling or explaining such mysteries, or riddles, that surround the lifeways of different people.

The customary way of learning these lifeways or cultures is to actually live *with* the people, doing what they do, learning their

1

rules, and their rules to break rules, by participating in and observing their day-to-day living. To actually *learn* the new culture means you must become as a child, learning to adjust, to participate, to survive. Sometimes this learning is exciting, other times, boring, and occasionally, dangerous.

The ideal time for an anthropologist, or fieldworker, to spend in the field is a whole year, which allows the fieldworker to participate in all the holidays, the seasons, the various events, the rituals and rites of passage in a society. However, many times this is impossible, so the research must be *focused* on the many facets of a whole culture: the social institutions of family, religion, education, power and prestige, economics, and health. First, the fieldworker must learn the language in order to understand the symbols, the rules of behavior, the belief systems, and the diverse patterns of life in that culture. Learning takes place by participating in as many life events as possible: births, funerals, marriages, civic and religious celebrations, whatever seems notable and whatever is made possible. Second, the ethnographer (fieldworker) must decipher the various roles of the people within the culture, as accurately as possible in terms of what is happening within a society at a particular time. For instance, how do females differ from males in their specific roles in a society? Or what behavior is appropriate for older women, or prepubescent females, or pregnant women, or for children? Or what do women of various statuses, such as those married to mayors, or widows of wealthy men, do in respect to specific events? Or what can you know by observing the behavior of the poorest-of-the-poor families? Or what can you find out about the behavior of ostracized women, such as prostitutes? Both men and women are included in the ethnographer's fieldwork, but because I am female, I am often able to study men only by observing or asking questions, as sometimes it is inappropriate for me to participate in certain male activities.

And in addition to a general description of the culture, fieldworkers may seek answers to specific questions, as I did about family formation. I wanted to know the reasons for having a large family in such a poverty-stricken area and what factors went into a family's decision-making process in forming their family. And I wondered if the child-rearing practices shape children to continue in these same decision-making processes.

As a fieldworker first enters a new culture, all symbols, mores, and rules seem fuzzy, strange, or indistinguishable, but as time goes by and with deep reflection, patterns of the lifeways become more clear, and understanding begins. It is important to remember that cultures are ever changing and adapting, so that rules and behaviors are also changing. It is impossible to gain a *complete* understanding, but an honest, dedicated fieldworker can do much to add to our knowledge about different lifeways. The anthropologist, after completing the field study, writes an account of that research; this account is called an ethnography—a picture from the people's points of view. It is through this ethnography that the story of a particular society comes alive and engages and informs the reader.

In this ethnography, *To the Mountain and Back*, I tell about the lives of people in a subsistence, peasant agricultural society from two different sides of the same coin. One side is Ladino and the other is Cakchiquel Mayan Indian, who live only ten kilometers apart in hoe-and-machete societies in the highlands of Guatemala. I take the reader through a period of discovery about how a stranger begins to function within a strange culture, to the growing awareness of the cultural fabric that binds each society into a functioning whole, and then finally toward an understanding of how these microcultures fit within the larger culture of Guatemala, a developing country.

In gaining perspective on understanding these peasant societies, I reach back into the rich history of the Maya who occupied the area before the Spanish Conquest, and I try to learn how this past still affects the present and will affect the future. I look also at the cultural beliefs and practices that the Spaniards brought to the New World which still retain an influence within these microcultures. I hope, through this process of discovery and reflection, to entice readers to use a similar process in researching the mysteries and riddles of other cultures.

My understanding of these people took place over a five-year period (1971–76) and in three separate phases: the first phase took place in 1971 in an Indian hospital and a remote clinic in the Department of Chimaltenango, Guatemala, during a six-week period when I worked as a volunteer nurse and a beginning doctoral student in anthropology. Three years later, in 1974, I began the second phase, my dissertation fieldwork, an ethnographic study based on living eight months in Zaragoza, a Ladino town, and in Patzún, an Indian town. During this time I focused broadly on sociocultural issues but also narrowly on the mystery of family formation. In addition to the ethnographic fieldwork, I did a randomized sample household survey of reproduction in each of the towns using a questionnaire I had developed. For this part of the work I had the help of two paid, trained interviewers. After finishing the fieldwork and analyzing the reproductive data, I returned yet another time, in 1975. During this third phase, I spent

several months doing further fieldwork and family studies in order to gain more information about the relationships between men and women and family decision making. I concluded that family reproduction and child-rearing practices in the towns were specific to the changing sociocultural needs of a hoe-and-machete subsistence agricultural society, Patzún, and an emerging, low-level cash economy in the other, Zaragoza.

The actual names of the towns are used in this study, as permission to do so was received from the towns' leaders. Copies of the original dissertation were given, in English, to a leader in each town. Names of all participants in the ethnography have been changed to protect their anonymity. I have used the real names of persons involved in my personal life, when possible with their permission, but when not possible, I hope with their endorsement.

An epilogue describes what has happened to the towns since 1976, to the people in Guatemala, to some of the people in this study, and to me, the researcher, during these subsequent years.

The first part of the ethnography begins with my undertaking a new role—missionary nurse in the Behrhorst Clinic and Hospital in Chimaltenango, Guatemala, May 17, 1971.

Chapter 2

A Man with a Mission

In the beginning . . . God gave to every people a cup,
a cup of clay, and from this cup they drank their life.
—Ruth Benedict, *Cups of Clay*, 1934

It is incredible that I would return to these mountains, time and again, now for over two decades. Recalling the first time—the smell of the burning timbers, when precious soil was being laid bare for yet another crop of sacred corn and the skies foretold the crashing rains of yet another monsoonal season—I can hardly believe that only I seem to have changed during these twenty years. The highlands of Guatemala still hold the secrets of the Mayan gods; the land still goes hungry, so overused, as the displaced indigenous people cope with their daily lives of hoe-and-machete agriculture, and women with wombs full of hope still have arms filled with the ache of another hungry child. Yet, the mystery of life continues, unrelenting and resounding, a scoff at those with less courage and a snub to those of less will. The bravery I encountered, lived, feared, and cherished is but a shadow of the greatness of the people in these haunting hills, with the dawning of yet another challenging tomorrow.

The Beginning

In the summer of 1971, I began a journey to the Land of Eternal Spring, Guatemala, with two motives in mind: to survive without

7

To the mountain . . . and back . . . serenity . . . eternity

my children, husband, kin; and to grow beyond my limited experience as a budding anthropologist in a land I had only read about and of which I knew so little. I had learned in my first semester of doctoral studies in cultural anthropology that to become a bona fide anthropologist one needed to spend time, the ideal year, in an unfamiliar cultural setting. Serendipitously during this year, a medical missionary, Dr. Carroll Behrhorst, had come to Denver, Colorado, seeking support for a program of health and development among the Cakchiquel (sometimes spelled Kaqchikel) Mayan Indians of Guatemala. He presented his plea for financial and other support to many groups around the United States. I was in one of these audiences when he asked for help.

Doc (as he was called) was a short, cherub-sort of man from Winfield, Kansas, who in 1959 had taken his family—wife and six children—to answer the call from the Lutheran church for a medical missionary to establish health care for the impoverished Indians in the highlands of Guatemala. Even in 1971 it was very clear that he was a man intent on changing the face of medical missions. I heard him say, "I am a man with a mission—a mission to change the way we deliver health care to the needy. From the Mayans, we have learned lessons on how to break the back of disease . . . not by merely curing the sick but rather by tackling the problems that have *caused* the sickness. We have to understand the people first, to know their way of life . . . to respect them. From this perspective we can gear our services to what the people want and need—to empower them."

He continued, "There are urgent medical needs—curative needs for these people cut off from their fertile lands by coffee plantation owners. They have one of the highest infant mortality rates in the world and also are one of the lowest per capita income nations." Hearing this message, three other nurses and I volunteered to go and help Doc in his new model of health care for these Mayan peoples. We were supported by the local Lutheran churches that provided each of us with about $500 for our airfare; we were to go one at a time, spending six weeks helping Doc in his Indian hospital. There was to be no overlap time between our volunteered times; in this way we could help Doc for almost six months.

I longed to go, not only to serve in this mission, which was a great desire, but also to get a taste of fieldwork in a foreign culture. But how could I go? I had an eight-year-old son and a five-year-old daughter, plus a husband who needed me. To leave for such a length of time and go into a place so strange was unthinkable. Yet I yearned for the chance. Bravely, I discussed this opportunity with my family one evening. My husband, Don, said, "Why not?" and the kids chimed in, "Sure, Mom!" Neither I nor they knew that this change in our lives would have such permanent effects.

I worked hard getting ready for this experience. I studied Spanish day and night, teaching myself to read and write, but never in a formal class, so I didn't have an opportunity to *hear and speak* the language. As my plans were taking shape for the anticipated fieldwork and experience, things were not going well with the volunteer plan to help Doc. Two of the other three volunteers had gone to Chimaltenango and subsequently returned to Denver; they were disappointed in what mission work was being done. The third volunteer, now in Guatemala, wrote me a long, sad letter about the fact that Doc didn't want any more "do-gooders," as he called us. She described the calamity as a misguided mission: Doc had found the volunteers disruptive to the lifestyles of the indigenous people. I was not to come!

I was devastated upon receiving this letter. Yet I took one more chance. I wrote directly to Dr. Behrhorst, explaining who I was, a doctoral student in anthropology. I was different! I wanted to work beside him to promote his vision—his dream. Weeks passed. I held my breath, and then one day I received a letter from Doc. It contained one sentence—*"You may come, but you are not welcome."* My heart sank, as brave and daring as I was I didn't believe I could face such a cold reception. What could I do? How could I manage in a strange country without language skills? How could I survive? All these questions and more flooded my mind. Yet from somewhere I found the courage to pick up my suitcase and head southward to Guatemala.

Crossing the Boundary: A Journey Begins

It was especially hard leaving my children the morning of May 17, 1971, as it was the beginning of their summer vacation, and we had many plans for picnics and fun. Up at 4:00 A.M., I kissed each good-bye as they slept, and my husband drove me to the airport. Neither of us said a word. I think we somehow knew it would never be the same. There are moments in one's life when you know that you have crossed a boundary and can never return the same again. The flight to Houston was uneventful, yet leaving the soil of the United States left me weak and sentimental. As the jet swooped down between the volcanoes and into the heart of the capital of Guatemala, I knew I was in another world.

People, people *everywhere*—and all speaking Spanish—very quickly. Struggling with my self-taught Spanish, the customs agents were patient as I produced the proper papers. As I waited for my luggage to arrive, people milled around and I felt lost. My tongue couldn't produce a sound in Spanish. It was nearly overwhelming. I grasped onto each word, hoping I wouldn't make a fatal mistake. In the midst of the turmoil at the airport, I thought I heard my name called—"Jody, Jody, Jody." No, it must be a mistake.

Yet I heard it again, from somewhere above. Glancing up toward the ceiling, I saw a large group of people looking down from a balcony. I saw no one I knew, yet I heard my name called again. Then I saw her. Could it be my friend Sally? Could it be? Yes, it was Sally, the volunteer nurse who, I thought, had already returned to Denver the day before I was to arrive. Tears came to my eyes; it seemed like a miracle. Now all my fears about how I was to get to Chimaltenango dissipated. I was saved. Grabbing my suitcase, I quickly escaped out into the street.

Sally came running down the stairs and we hugged.

"I couldn't get out like I planned, as the immigration office messed up my papers; so I'm leaving in the morning," Sally shouted.

Walking at a slower pace down the stairs came a blonde man with a mustache—no smile. He had on cotton pants and a white short-sleeved shirt. "I want you to meet John," said Sally. "He's Doc's right-hand man; he's a Peace Corps volunteer."

"Glad to meet you," I mumbled, rather surprised to meet another American so soon.

"I'm giving you a lift to Chimaltenango." John spoke tersely, with a New York accent.

I was relieved. "Thanks, I really appreciate your help," I gasped. John and I moved toward a large van, as Sally waved good-bye.

"You'll be all right," she called, "I'll see you in Denver—in six weeks." With that quick departure, my last connection with home disappeared into the crowd.

"I have to pick up some supplies before we head back," John said, again tersely. The old van sped across several lanes of traffic and through alleys, parkways, honking horns, walking people, sliding people with carts, crippled people, women with children on their backs in slings, horses, bicycles, dogs, and men with machine guns. The blur of human activity, the smell of the city, the noise of the traffic—like none I'd ever encountered before—this was the beginning of my foreign experience. This was my introduction to Guatemala.

And this was John, the Peace Corps volunteer, who was to teach me so much, yet never let me know who *he* was. John was a mystery man who had served in Vietnam, at the very beginning of the conflict. He had distrustful blue eyes, a sandy mustache and sandy hair, a muscular build. He had worked with Doc as a Peace Corps volunteer for two years, had recently married a woman from Nebaj, Guatemala, and now they had an infant daughter. I remembered these brief descriptions from the letters I had received from Sally, my missionary friend.

"I suppose you're one of those do-gooders," was the first thing John said as we headed up a steep mountain incline, away from the bustling city. "Or are you down here to sightsee like some of the others?"

Dumbfounded, yet challenged, I replied, "I'm neither. I'm here to learn about the people—and maybe something about myself."

The conviction in my voice must have startled John, for he looked straight at me; his piercing eyes went through me as he said, "I think you're right—and you *will* learn."

"Can you tell me about some of the places we're seeing?" I asked softly. "I really want to learn."

As the van clung to the sides of the mountain, and as we bounced along around blind curves, passing smoking trucks on the right side of the road with seconds to safety, John began to tell me about the sights we were seeing. "You see the volcanoes smoking?" John asked.

"Yes, they're beautiful. Are they dangerous?" I remarked.

"They can be, but they haven't been for some time. They do some good, as the ash fertilizes the soil. The land is so overworked by these poor people, anything helps. The rains will start any day now; you'll see how the people plant every inch of land. They're starving, you know. The best land in the highlands was given to woodsmen from Germany, around the turn of the century, so these woodsmen could plant coffee trees and make a lot of money. But none of it has gone to the native people, the Mayan Indians. In fact, they just got pushed from their land and had to move higher and higher onto the land that was less and less fertile; now that's all they have." Bitterness crept into his voice. "They don't even have wood for cooking and for keeping warm," he sighed. I, too, was to learn about the land-hunger of these people, how they were to scratch the land for food to grow and to huddle together for warmth in the damp, cold nights of the rainy season. I was to see infants and children die from bronchopneumonia with few antibodies to fight the infections because of malnutrition and poor living quarters.

"See the smoke over there?" John pointed eastward. "That's what is known as slash-and-burn agriculture."

"Yes, I've read about it and of all the problems this type of farming creates. The land just becomes more and more barren. How can you stop that practice?"

"You can't when people are hungry. But we try to teach them at Doc's to rotate the crops, to let some of it lie fallow for a season or two without planting, and to make deeper ditches, about three-feet deep, so that water holds and doesn't wash the topsoil away. Commercial fertilizers help the barren soil, and they have been strong here, lately, but they cost a lot, so the farmers don't make much on their crops. It's a pretty vicious cycle."

We had now climbed higher into the mountains, where the air was fresher and cooler. The trees were fewer, and the land stretched between the rugged peaks. Fewer people were walking on the side of the highway, but there still were many. The colorful clothing that women were wearing was new to me.

"Have you noticed all the different *huipiles*?" asked John.

"What are those?" I responded.

"Huipiles are the blouses that women weave in their villages. Each one is distinct from each village, so you can tell right away where they're from. You know there are about 200 different dialects of the five major Mayan languages spoken here in Guatemala, so people have trouble understanding one another. Their huipiles are at least one way of telling where they're from. My favorite is Nebaj; it's blue and violet. Of course, that's where my wife is from!" John laughed. He was more relaxed and teaching me what he loved.

"I see some people with just regular shirts and pants, too. Who are they?" I asked.

"Those are the Ladinos. Most of the time you don't see many, unless they're young, in the highlands. They stay mostly in Guatemala City (referred to as the City) or on the coasts. About half the people in Guatemala are Indian (called natives, indigenous, or *naturales*), and the other half are a mix of Indian and Spanish (called Ladino). Everything is run by Ladinos; they have all the power, except in some areas in the highlands. Part of the reason for that is that they can read and write in Spanish, so they can do business with others. The Indians don't have a written language [many do now, as I write in 1993], so they have to do their business without knowing a lot of what is going on. We're trying to change that, but it is slow, slow, slow. Kids don't go to school here like they do in the States; you'll see that. Girls hardly at all," John continued, getting excited about what he knew and seeing that I was really interested in those issues.

"You'll see that the Indians really love life, so simple; they call themselves naturales, the natural people. They take life as it comes—naturally; to them, family is the most important thing. But without the land, it's hard to keep the family together, as the Indian men have to go to the coast to work in the harvest. They also have to go into Guatemala City to get work for cash, so they have to learn Spanish. That's when they become Ladino. Sometimes they go only for the week as a Ladino, but sometimes they find it just easier to stay Ladino. Then their wives and children give up their old ways, too, and become Ladino. I really hate to see it happen, it makes me sad, but that's the way life is," John summarized.

This small conversation put into perspective what I had read in Eric Wolf's *Sons of the Shaking Earth* (1959) and Richard Adams's *Crucifixion by Power* (1970). Adams points out that in order to understand the poverty of various regions in Guatemala, one needs to understand the larger society. In order to understand this larger system, one needs to understand the microsystem—that of the family, the kinship system, and how it is related to the entire society. It was this network, the family system, that I had come to study. I wanted to learn how the family economy related to the larger market. But the answers to those complex questions were far into the future. I was just beginning to assimilate the sights and smells of this, my field site.

A Town at the Crossroads

The sun was setting as we reached a crossroad with hundreds of people milling around. "This is the famous city of Chimaltenango, home for about 30,000 people," John said, sarcastically. "It's known as the continental divide of the country. The water runs either north or south from here. I think it's an ugly city. The people can't get along with each other. They come from all over—maybe that's one of the problems; they don't have roots." He pulled the van around a large green fountain into what appeared to be a plaza. Vendors were selling cotton candy, corn on the cob, and sausages. Again, there were many children with bare feet, mothers with more babies on their backs, and dogs lapping up garbage. The noise was high-pitched—people shouting, calling out for one another, selling their wares, getting ready for the night; horns were honking, bells were ringing. NOISE!

A cloud of dust followed us everywhere.

"I'll take you to the pension," John said. (He used the word by which boardinghouses are known in Guatemala.)

I half heard him, because my head was spinning so. I had no idea where I was; I just knew I was a long way from home. But this was to be my home for six weeks—Chimaltenango, one of twenty-two departments in the Republic of Guatemala, one of the largest of the

Central American countries. In Chimaltenango, Indians, the Cakchiquel Mayan, make up over three-fourths of the population; it is a center of Indian power. The Department of Chimaltenango (also called the western highlands) was 77.6 percent Indian at the time of my first visit (Adams, 1970:127). Although only forty kilometers west of Guatemala City, Chimaltenango seems a world away; it is physically and culturally vastly different from the City. The old van that John had driven so recklessly through the mountains had left the Valley of Guatemala, at an altitude of about 5,000 feet above sea level to where we were now, at 6,200 feet. The palm trees of Guatemala City had given way to the oak, pine, and cypress trees of the highlands. The remote, isolated hamlets along the way had consisted of cane huts with thatched roofs; now, in Chimaltenango, they were replaced by a city of adobe. Adobe mud, cheap and easy to find, is used to construct the typical home in the highlands. The mud bricks are dried in the hot, tropical sun; many are made without straw filling to hold them together, so when the rains come, the houses sometimes simply melt away. The nights can be very cool, even frosty at this altitude. The seasons are divided into two: the wet, which is monsoonal, and the dry. The dry season begins sometime in late October and lasts until mid-May, when the wet season begins.

A screech of the brakes, and I knew I had arrived at La Bohemia, the boardinghouse in which I would rent a room for fifteen dollars a month (in Guatemalan money, fifteen *quetzales*). I found the meals too expensive, so I ate very few of them in La Bohemia. "See you at 7:00 A.M. at the hospital," was the last word from my escort, John.

"Thanks for the lift," I called out as the van swirled around and headed back toward the center of town. There I stood alone, suitcase in hand, staring into the yard of a squat-looking house with red-tiled roof, surrounded by cyprus and pine trees. There were chairs and tables on the lawn; a small iron gate led into a patio. I entered. Huddled in a corner was a couple drinking coffee, engaged in conversation. Stumbling through a darkened hallway, I came into a small, dimly lit dining room. There were five tables. Everything was dark—the tables, the piano in the corner, even the paintings on the walls. But the smell was pure bakery. It smelled of chocolate cake, pies, abundant freshly baked bread, and rich coffee. La Bohemia, I had arrived. This cafe was not a place for gringos, but a favorite resting place for upper-class Guatemalans, in particular those of German or Norwegian ancestry. They would stop, not to spend the night, but for coffee, pastries, and gossip, on their way to or from their coffee *fincas* (farms). La Bohemia was established by Germans and Scandinavians who owned the coffee land along the way from Guatemala City. The present owner was a painter whose name was Olga, and she spoke English, so I was told. I could hardly wait to tell her of my arrival, to eat some of her famous cake, have a cup of coffee, and use the bathroom.

Waiting for what seemed an eternity, I finally called out, "Hello." No answer. Perhaps in Spanish? "*Hola.*" Still no answer. I made noise, shuffling my feet around. Yes, someone was coming! Around the corner came not Olga, but a very small Guatemalan girl. She looked at me with suspicion and said something—very rapidly.

"I am JoAnn; I have come from the United States to stay," I said in my best Spanish.

With that she looked even more puzzled, and I was not sure that she understood me at all. Next, we both looked for help, but none came. Then the small girl, looking even more troubled, motioned me to follow her. Up, up, up some dark stairs we went. At the top, she opened a door to what appeared to be an attic room. I entered and saw what was to be my room for the next six weeks: one light (a bare bulb on an electric cord), a floor of bare boards, and clinging to one of the slanting sides of the room, a flat surface of boards that appeared to be the bed. There were also a small wooden chest of drawers, a wire on which to hang my clothes, a thin, striped pad for the board-bed, and a floor-level window about twenty-four inches square that looked out onto a red-tiled roof. There was no chair.

The small Guatemalan girl began speaking very quickly again. I didn't know what she was saying. Then her arms flailed about. I kept smiling. She tried again. I smiled. With a disgusted look on her face, she left. I stood dumbfounded in the middle of the room holding my suitcase. Within minutes the door opened again, and the small girl entered with a bundle of bedding, a blanket, pillow, and sheets. Dumping these onto the board-bed, she left. I then understood that she had been asking me if I wanted some bedding. The beginning of understanding a new culture comes when two people make an encounter and reach a mutual solution. I had a lot to learn.

Picking up the bundle, I arranged it in some fashion on the board-bed. I hung some of my few belongings—a white uniform, a blue-and-white-striped uniform, a sweater, a skirt, and a pantsuit—on the wire. My other things—a precious camera, tape recorder and Spanish dictionary—went into the chest of drawers with the picture of my children, Paul and Janis, and my husband, Don, placed on it. I was unpacked. I now needed a bathroom and food. With courage I crept down the steep stairs and peered around corners and finally found a bathroom with a small sink and toilet. After using the toilet,

I washed my face with water from a small bucket, using only my hand and letting my face dry by itself, as there was no towel. A small mirror of waves and curves above the sink gave me little hope of ever seeing myself for six weeks. But then I would learn that this was almost a gift. A person in the field doesn't look the way he or she has learned to expect himself or herself to look.

I was so hungry. The last meal had been somewhere over Mexico, and that seemed like years ago. Although I could smell the bakery, I never saw anyone to ask for a meal—or anything. The only thing edible that I had brought along in my suitcase was a small bag of butterscotch drops. Famished, I ate them all. Throughout my years in the field, I learned that getting adequate, edible food can really be a problem. I began to take granola bars (sometimes called energy bars) along and to purchase bananas along the way—with the outside peel, they were safe to eat. Obtaining water was usually the biggest problem, as most supplies were unsafe. Even with the greatest precautions, water supplies were always suspect.

Sleep came quickly; I was exhausted. I didn't need an alarm clock then (or at any time during the fieldwork), because the pesky roosters of Guatemala began their wakeup calls at about four o'clock in the morning, each one more eager than the other to greet the day. They were amazingly noisy. It was still rather dark in the room, because of the small window, but I decided to get up, since I was very hungry. I went quickly to the bathroom to prepare for my first day as a voluntary missionary nurse. This time there was hardly *any* water in the bucket, perhaps a cupful. I used my washcloth to dampen my face and body, realizing that this was what was meant by a "spit bath." Lacking water, the toilet didn't flush. There seemed to be so little water anywhere. This was my first experience in understanding the dry season, and I began to understand why the Maya, Aztecs, and Incas all worshiped rain gods so much.

Dressed in my white uniform and white shoes, I was ready to find the hospital. Again I saw no one in the restaurant to ask for food, so I decided to walk toward the center of town. Before I had time to deliberate about which direction to begin walking, I heard my name called. Again—was I hallucinating?—no, it was distinctly my name! Peeking out the small window I saw the sturdy figure of a woman in a blue dress that looked like a uniform. She was waving and calling my name. I knew immediately it must be Edith Sherwood, the British midwife that I had heard so much about. I hurried down the stairs and out to the patio to meet her.

"I'm glad to meet you; I've heard so much about you from the other nurses! I didn't expect to see you today, as John said that you were out of town," I said excitedly.

Edith, the British midwife, and John, the Peace Corps volunteer, ponder the daily problems of the hospital

"Oh, John. He always wants to be in charge. Come on, we have a long way to go." She did not ask me whether I had had breakfast or anything to eat, so I tried to fake strength, as I walked briskly with my British colleague. As we walked, people greeted her; she spoke to everyone. Edith chattered on about the working relationship with John and also about some of her more exciting experiences at the hospital. I saw so much on that walk of about one mile. Chimaltenango was similar to Guatemala City; except for a few motorcycles, nothing in Chimaltenango was motorized. People were beasts of burden. First, I saw men carrying great loads of wood, rope, and food on their backs and heads. Some men and younger boys were pulling large, wooden cargo carts through the dirt streets. Their feet were bare as they dug into the dusty road. They increased the leverage by putting leather straps across their foreheads, like harnesses. They laughed and had seemingly great energy. Women, too, carried large bundles of food, firewood, and cloth on their heads; their babies were slung on their backs or in front, breastfeeding; they walked quickly down the dusty roads. I saw people nibbling on fruit or candies as they walked along. Perhaps they, too, were hungry, like me, and couldn't take time to sit and eat. Or maybe they didn't have the money for a full breakfast and so kept the pangs of hunger diminished somewhat by eating the small snack. Every place was dusty.

Edith explained in her British accent, "Today is a quiet day in Chimaltenango, as it isn't a market day. We have market days on Tuesdays, Fridays, and Sundays—every town has different days for market, so that they pass the sales around. When you come down tomorrow, you won't be able to walk down the street; it will be filled with people selling everything you can imagine. It's a happy day, because you get to see your family and friends. Sometimes there are fireworks and music."

The market system is the basis of the Guatemalan peasant economy, a complex network system. As Richard Adams (1970) described the network, "it is an extremely delicate system, and its very responsiveness to the changes in the natural and cultural environments makes it difficult to handle" (14). Studying this delicate market system would be a goal of this research.

"You're supposed to meet Doc this morning after he finishes the rounds he makes at the hospital. You know we don't deliver babies—that's all done in the home by midwives—and we don't do any surgery here. We have all sorts of sick people here. Doc goes to every patient's bed, all 100 or so, every morning and then comes down again at night at about seven. Besides the hospital, we see about 30,000 patients in the clinic every year. By now there will be about 100 lined up to see him, and on market day there are more," Edith explained.

"I'm really looking forward to seeing him again," I said hesitantly, knowing I wasn't welcome. "Have you been here long?" I asked.

"I came about two years ago, and wouldn't be anywhere else. Doc is really incredible. There is so much poverty here. Sometimes I think I can't see another baby die; yet I stay on. You know half of the kids die before they are five years old," Edith said. I shuddered, thinking of my own five-year-old daughter. "If we could just have enough food for them," Edith continued. "There are so many infections they get, but they can't fight them, because they don't have the antibodies built up. They just don't get enough protein. But Doc, his plans always include helping the people get and keep their land, so that they can grow more food. He has a whole system of agriculture, safe water projects, and now is working on getting the people to start cooperatives so that they can buy their seed together, sell together, and in this way get ahead. His other big program in development is the *promotores de salud* [health promoters]," Edith finished.

"Tell me more," I urged.

"These are men, mostly, who are chosen by leaders of their villages to study medicine in order to give simple care to the people. We teach them here to recognize the symptoms for simple sicknesses, like the flu, bronchitis, diarrheal stuff, malaria. We teach them what simple and safe drugs can be given; then if they see something serious, they have that sick person brought into the hospital to see Doc. Every week the promotores come to the hospital and make rounds with Doc; he checks their abilities to diagnose and treat various symptoms. He evaluates whether they are doing the right things, and so forth, and I teach them new things, too. When the promotores finish the course, we give them a certificate that they put on the wall of their office in the village. The promotores can buy medicine at cost at the hospital, but they have to sell the drugs at cost, too, to the people in their villages. Promotores can't make money on selling the medicine; they just recover the cost. This is a system of *the people*. There are now about fifty promotores that we have trained, and Doc is planning to train more. He also teaches them about new crops to grow and also how to read and write.

"Doc hopes that some day a few of these promotores will go to the University Medical School in Guatemala City, so that someday the Indians will be educated and able to take over the whole Behrhorst Hospital and Development Program. That's his goal, but it's so hard to get the money to support the plan. So you can see Doc really is concerned that the right people come here who understand his mission." Edith had summarized what the Behrhorst Program was all about and why it was important to understand his mission—and not to come as a "do-gooder." I was glad I was to become a part of it, even if I wasn't welcome. By this time we had arrived at the wall of a large compound. "This is it," said Edith, to my surprise.

As we entered the walled compound, the startling picture of this hospital, unlike any other I had seen or imagined, surrounded us. The patio, or courtyard, was filled with activity: people were scrubbing wheelchairs, others were scrubbing mattresses; vendors were selling hot tortillas and mush; women were carrying babies on their backs and buckets in their hands; nurses dressed in colorful Indian huipiles with white aprons over them were walking quickly with trays of medicines and jugs of hot cereal. The smell of smoke was everywhere (and still lingers in my mind more than twenty years later). Some children were playing marbles on the patio floor;

Behrhorst Chimaltenango Hospital where the harmony of life and death emerges

people looked happy in spite of this being a hospital. The red-tiled roof was similar to what I had seen of their native homes, and the white stucco walls were also homelike. And the place was open, so different from the closed-in hospitals of the United States.

A white-aproned nurse in the colorful native dress, black hair pulled neatly into a bun, walked out to meet us. "Hello, I am Margarita, the head nurse." She spoke clearly, and slowly, making sure that I understood her. Her face looked like those of Mayan women I had seen in textbooks. "Let me introduce you to the other nurses," she continued. Names became a blur, as each greeted me, speaking quickly. Five were in the native dress of reds, blues, and yellows with a wraparound skirt of the same colors. There were three women dressed in plain white uniforms, such as I had on. I was later to learn that those in white uniforms were the Ladinos; they were lesser in rank in this Indian hospital. After trying to grasp this new situation, I was touched on the arm by one of the Ladino nurses who pointed me to the outside patio and motioned me to follow her. I did. We went from room to room with her explaining to me, slowly, what kinds of patients were in the hospital. Large rooms contained small hospital cots on which several people were sometimes lying together. "Families," she said. I understood. Under each cot I could see pots and pans, and bedding as well. I remembered Doc had explained his philosophy of care: to heal, you need

Cakchiquel Mayan nurse prepares Western-style medicines

to have your loved ones *with* you, so they come. Also, the hospital did not furnish food, only a nutritional drink and a mush, so every family cooked for itself. In some ways it seemed like a circus with so many people milling around, but the philosophy makes a lot of sense. The windows were open for fresh air, and the cement floors were kept clean. Doc had once said, "You can keep a person clean and comfortable, but only his family can really give him love." This is probably why the hospital continues to be a thriving, loving place for the Indian people.

As we continued on our tour of the hospital, the Ladino nurse took me to one room toward the outside of the building. As we entered, I could feel the heat and see the open flames of a large cooking area. The cooking surface was a metal sheet supported by cinder blocks on a waist-high cement table. Families were busy cooking breakfast. I was to learn that here was where I was to boil water for many of the treatments we gave in the hospital. In modern hospitals this room would have been called a utility room; here it was both that and a kitchen for the families.

When Doc first came from Winfield, Kansas, he hired a nurse from Guatemala City to help him train five illiterate Guatemalan girls to become his staff nurses. These five women have continued working for Doc and have trained yet more nurses. During my six weeks of work with them, I found that these nurses were well trained and very dedicated. The nursing care given here was simple, but very good.

Next we came to a large room filled with children. The nurse said simply, "These are the starving children. Most don't live." I knew I was seeing the face of poverty and malnutrition once again. These scenes etched in my mind the need to study the subject of reproduction. Why would families continue to have children when so few could live? This was the riddle to be solved; it was a cultural pattern that to me was a mystery, yet one I would learn to understand.

As we finished the tour, Edith, the British midwife, came running to us, saying, "Doc wants to meet you."

My heart sank. Now I had to confront the issue that I wasn't welcome. With head held high, I followed Edith through the corridor and around to another courtyard, the clinic, where a long line of Indian women, children, and some men were waiting to see Doc. We went in quickly.

I could hear the voice of a man speaking Spanish with a Kansan accent emanating from behind a curtain. He would ask a question, pause, show concern, listen to the soft Indian answer, question some more, pause, and so on, until both he and the patient were satisfied. His phrases conveyed a strong sense of commitment, objectivity, and professionalism. Soon that patient was getting off the examining table, and another was entering, while Doc scribbled on a prescription pad. He poked his head around the curtain and said, "Well, you got here!"

"Yes. Thanks for the lift in the ambulance," I replied.

"Do you speak Spanish?" was his next question.

"Not very well," I replied honestly.

"Well, get out there and start talking to the people," he said abruptly. With that the doctor went back behind the curtain and began the next examination, his Kansan accent again filling the room. I knew an ordeal was over; I had had my meeting with Doc.

"Let's grab a cup of coffee," Edith said.

I couldn't believe my ears. I wondered if anyone knew how hungry I really was—how thin I must have become!

We hurried across the street where I had come the night before; motorcycles, buses, and carts were now a mass of action. We entered a small store, a *tienda*. Toward the back of the store were

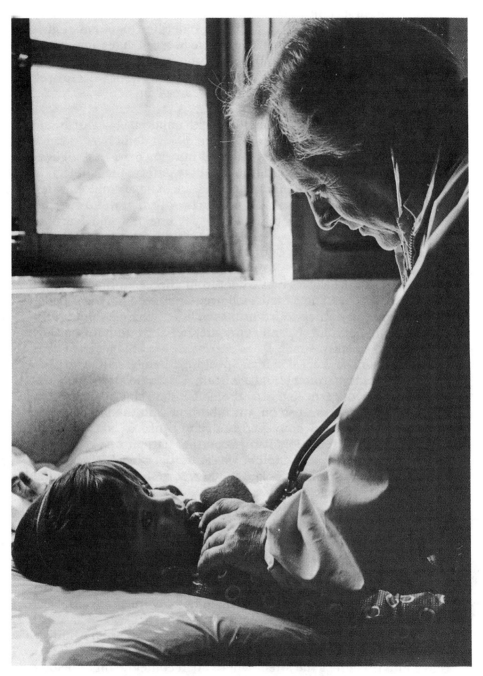

Dr. Carroll Behrhorst, founder of the Chimaltenango Development Program, with a patient

three small tables with chairs. We ordered black coffee, and Edith explained, "If you don't say *negro*, they'll fill it with lots of sugar." We also ordered a sandwich of some type of luncheon meat. "I watch what I eat, because I have been sick three times this year; and don't drink the water," warned Edith. It was the best sandwich I had eaten in years!

Young men came around our table. I couldn't understand their remarks, but I could tell they were flirting. "You're quite an attraction to them," Edith explained. "You're so tall and blonde; they are very curious about you." I felt uncomfortable, not knowing whether to talk with them or ignore them; I learned through the years to be polite, but not inviting, as I respected their curiosity but wanted a clear role distinction, that of being a serious foreigner, a researcher.

We had hardly finished our coffee and sandwich when a boy ran into the tienda, hurried to Edith and began speaking rapidly; I couldn't understand him. Edith looked perplexed and then said, "There's been a death of a twelve-year-old boy. He came in last night to the hospital with lockjaw, and we couldn't save him. Doc wants me to go with his family to take his body to his home—150 kilometers from here. It's a long, hard drive, and we need to reach his village before sundown. You know the Indians have a custom of burying the dead the day they die—before sundown. It's a long drive, and we can barely make it; do you want to ride along?"

"I'm really sorry about the family's loss; it must be hard on them. Yes, if it wouldn't be any bother, I'd like to ride along."

"Then follow me, and we'll find out the details."

We found that the dead boy—nearly a grown man in this area—was the only son of an older couple. He had received a bad cut on his foot from a machete; he cleaned the cut, but he hadn't had an immunization for tetanus. When the symptoms of lockjaw set in, the family had tried to get to the hospital in time, but it was a long way, and even by bus, they got there too late. Doc said, "This is a real tragedy for this family. The boy was their social security; he soon would have had the major responsibility for farming and bringing in some income. Usually children die before they are five—of diarrhea or measles—but after five they are strong enough to fight off most infections until they are old. Boys usually marry at about eighteen years of age and start another family, so this death is a real blow to the mother and father, who are now in their late thirties and expect to live to about forty-five or fifty, really only about ten or fifteen more years."

A crowd had gathered around the room where the body of the boy lay. Two young men came in, carrying a simple wooden coffin.

It was too small, so they had to find another, larger one. Sadness surrounded the hospital. I knew the statistics about half the children dying before the age of five, but this case was in a way more tragic. I stood silently, trying to think of ways of expressing my sympathy; death is a shared sorrow among all people.

Edith disappeared. The family was crying and talking in Cakchiquel, the language of this region. The other four major Mayan languages of Guatemala are: Mom, Pokomom, Ixjual, and Quiché. Each language represents a different tribe. The languages have a basic similarity in that they are tonal languages, but each is distinct from the others. Soon Edith reappeared, driving the ambulance-van that John had used the day before to pick me up in Guatemala City. She discussed the situation with the family, and six people got into the back; the coffin containing the young boy's body was slid in between their legs. They all were somber, stoic.

"We have to get gas and then be on the road as quickly as possible," Edith said sternly. We stopped and filled the gasoline tank and soon were on the paved highway again. During the four-hour trip, Edith drove the ambulance with confidence. As we drove through the mountains, Edith talked a lot about the experiences she had had during her two years with the program. She described the times when Doc was out of the country—she was the "physician" in charge of the whole hospital.

"Of course the Guatemalan officials don't like that," she said, "so we get another doctor from the City to 'cover' my decisions, but he isn't kind, and the Indians don't like him, so they leave the hospital and go home. They know when they are respected or not; that's why Doc is their hero. He respects them."

As we continued higher and higher into the mountains, each curve brought greater beauty. The volcanic mountains hugged the sky, while the lushness of the trees, even in the dry season, was majestic in a land that was cultivated long before the Spanish Conquest. "Let's stop for something to drink," Edith suggested, since it was past noon by then. We spotted a little store around the curve, drove in, and stopped. There I had a new lesson in social customs. There was no *sanitario* (latrine), so the men relieved themselves by the side of the ambulance. We women went into the bush. Women and small girls in the highlands are always very modest.

After a quick drink, we again were back on the highway; the shadows were growing longer when we finally turned off the paved highway and onto a dusty, dirt road. We drove only about a kilometer before we came to a walled area. "We're here," Edith sighed. We drove through an opening in the wall and into a plaza lined with several hundred people.

"Just as I thought," exclaimed Edith. "They knew we were coming!"

"What do you mean?" I asked.

"It happens all the time. When we have someone die at the hospital, the folks in the villages *just know*; I don't know how they do, but they do. And when we get here, they are waiting, with the grave already dug. It's a mystery, as if they have a sixth sense or something."

I thought about that incident many times as the years went by. It was true. The people had no telephones or telegraphs in these remote areas, and they couldn't run as fast by foot as we traveled by ambulance, so how did they know? Many times in the years to come natives would ask me, "Why don't *you* know?" as if I had some type of defect; they seemed to be able to *just know* when people were coming to visit or when other events were about to occur.

"What will happen now?" I asked.

"They will take the coffin right to the grave and bury it; the Indians will bury beneath the ground, because they believe that is where they came from, but the Ladinos will bury above the ground in various types of mausoleums." For the most part I found this distinction to be true, but the basis of the decision of burying below ground or above might be wealth rather than worldview.

"After the burial, the women go into the house and cook, and the men get crazy drunk. They drink all night and sleep it off the next day," Edith concluded. I found this description to be quite accurate except in the larger settlements where a priest would say a few prayers and light some incense and candles at the burial site—a brief and simple ceremony. The immediate grieving period also is short, although the dead are honored throughout the years with periodic masses said to their memory. Indians do not wear black, only their regular dress, but the Ladino widows and widowers wear black. Both can remarry, but most do not. Most do not change their residence; however, for those who are alone, it is preferred that they move in with their married children.

This time, we didn't stay for the burial but headed back to Chimaltenango after the coffin was taken from the ambulance, as it was growing dark. It didn't take us long to return, since we were driving downhill most of the time. We arrived back in town at about eight in the evening. Edith invited me into her cottage for some stew, which I enjoyed, then I struggled to my room at about half past nine, exhausted from a day filled with new experiences and a trip into the hinterland. I was so tired that I didn't even think about being homesick. And so ended my first day in the field.

Chapter 3

The Face of Poverty

Sahagun is very explicit when he says that the first inhabitants
of New Spain landed in Panutla and traveled along the seacoast
looking toward the snow-covered mountains and volcanoes until
they came to the province of Guatemala.
—the Popul Vuh

I had learned so much in just twenty-four hours, my first day in
the Land of Eternal Spring, Guatemala, home of the mysterious
Mayan tribes, the place where Pedro de Alvarado, the tall, red-
headed conquistador, had defeated the Mayan Quiché kings. What
could I expect the second day?

Language: The Basic Skill of Fieldwork

There seemed to be no space between my first and second days
in the field, as crowing roosters and the first rays of morning seemed
to link the night into day. I judged it to be about six in the morning,
so I had about an hour to eat and get ready. Then I would walk a
mile to the hospital. I thought I'd better hurry. After a refreshing
quick splash in the bathroom sink, I dressed in my nurse's uniform
and went downstairs to the dining room. I sat expectantly at a small
table in the dimly lit dining room, waiting for a waiter. Eventually,
from around the corner, a slender young man appeared; I motioned
to him to come for my order. Then in Spanish I said, *"Me gustaría
tener un café negro, huevos revueltos, y pan, por favor"* (I'd like
to have black coffee, scrambled eggs, and bread, please).

29

There! I had done it; I had ordered my first meal, alone. Before many minutes went by, the slender man reappeared with a cup and saucer and a small chrome pitcher of steaming black coffee. Success! I thought. Moments later the young waiter brought another plate, but this was a puzzle. On it was a large piece of chocolate cake. What happened to my eggs and bread? I felt foolish and helpless, since knowing the local language and then speaking it clearly are basic skills in doing good fieldwork. I was to face embarrassment, inconvenience, and humor in the weeks ahead as I tried to communicate in a foreign language. Fieldworkers must decode the culture in which they are working and, like children, learn the rules and mores for the first time. Until the fieldworker and the culture become as one, they are likely to suffer many blunders.

Language is the first task to master in doing fieldwork in a foreign country—and the hardest. For this reason, before I began my dissertation fieldwork in 1974, I twice enrolled in a total immersion program at El Proyecto Lingüístico Marroquín, a language school in Antigua, Guatemala. The first time was in 1972, a year after my initial trip to Guatemala; the second time was in 1974, immediately before I began my fieldwork. A total immersion system, I believe, is the best way to learn a foreign language. Learning the language in this manner helps foreigners become familiar with local idioms and accents, thus preparing them to move with more ease into the local field.

After the humbling experience of receiving chocolate cake instead of bread and scrambled eggs, I carried my dictionary everywhere. During the evening hours I would tape-record myself speaking Spanish, so that I might improve my accent. I would also listen to the radio to familiarize myself with the rhythm and words of the language, and of course, I would try to speak with everyone, listening carefully, and asking them to speak slowly and be patient. People in Guatemala were especially kind and forbearing, listening to my early struggles in the language. Now I speak Spanish fluently, but as a *campesina* (a country girl), for it was in the rural setting that I learned to speak Spanish—the Indian-Spanish of the highlands of Guatemala.

Finishing my cake-and-coffee breakfast, I hurried to the cottage next door to meet Edith. Knocking several times, I heard no answer. Finally, I heard a faint voice, "I'm not feeling very well; you go ahead to the hospital," Edith called out.

"What do you think you have?" I asked.

"*El grippe*," (stomach flu) Edith replied. El grippe is the most common diarrheal disorder encountered by natives and tourists alike. It can be temporary (simple gastritis), or it may be more serious, such as with amoebic dysentery. A developing country brings foreigners face to face with all types of communicable diseases to which they have never been exposed before. (This can be particularly hazardous for those moving to hot climates, but that is not the case in the highlands of Guatemala.) Having some type of training in first aid and medical care is essential to remain healthy and productive. Many times fieldwork is cut short or terminated because of illness. I was often sick during my years of fieldwork, but I was hospitalized only once—for food poisoning. I learned it was most important to use precautions, all the time, being especially careful to maintain sanitary procedures in handling food and bathroom wastes.

In spite of her strong will, Edith's illness was serious; she had typhoid fever. Her fever rose, and she became delirious; she weakened quickly. Doc Behrhorst ordered her to stay in bed and put her on some antibiotics. During the rest of my six weeks, Edith never left her house. I helped her as I could, and other friends brought her food and did errands for her.

I felt very bad leaving Edith alone that morning as I trudged to the hospital by myself, wondering if I could manage without her— and also, being human, wondering whether I, too, would get sick (I didn't during those six weeks). At last I reached the hospital grounds, arriving about fifteen minutes late. This morning I was to meet the woman I had heard so much about—Magdelena.

Meeting Magdelena Katok: Cakchiquel Nurse

Magdelena Katok, a Cakchiquel Indian from the area, was one of the first nurses Doc had trained when he and his family arrived in Chimaltenango from Winfield, Kansas, in 1962. She had become a central force for the Behrhorst Program. A sensitive, intelligent, humorous woman about thirty years of age, Magdelena was committed to improving the lives of the Indians.

Entering the hospital compound, I went directly to the clinic, where Edith had told me I would find Magdelena. She was there twice a week, dispensing medicines and doing other treatments, and the other days she was the manager of a nursing clinic in a small village, Xajáxac, about four hours away by bus and at a much higher altitude (9,000 feet above sea level) than Chimaltenango (6,200 feet above sea level). I was to go with Magdelena to Xajáxac for the next six weeks, acting as her assistant, though obviously a naive pupil. I would learn much from Magdelena.

Entering the clinic I heard a soft but strong voice: "I'm

Magdelena." The words came from a woman who spoke with a wide, open, smiling face.

I stared and thought, Could she be Mayan? She was unlike any Mayan goddess I had ever seen pictured in textbooks. Her beautiful, large brown eyes, glistening smile, perfect teeth invited comfort and tranquility. I thought she looked Polynesian—like a Pacific Islander—she probably weighed 200 pounds and was about five feet tall. Her long black hair was pulled back into a thick braid; she was exquisite. It was very unusual for a Cakchiquel Indian to be overweight. With their almost vegetarian diet, scarce available food, and high level of physical activity, they don't have many extra calories for fat deposit. I was curious about this paradox.

"I have been eager to meet you," I spoke hesitantly. "All the other nurses from Denver told me of your kindness." Her facial expression told me she understood me. Magdelena was experienced in hearing strange accents and syntaxes from foreigners trying to speak Spanish for the first time. She also had been to the United States—Los Angeles—she later told me. I instantly relaxed, knowing I was understood.

"After I finish with the patients, we'll go and buy our food for our trip tomorrow," Magdelena said.

"I'm looking forward to that," I responded sincerely. She was busy with several patients standing in line. I didn't know what I was to do, so I said, "Do you mind if I sit here and watch what you do?"

"Please do." She smiled and seemed comfortable with having an audience.

"I want to learn about the treatments and the medicines that are used," I explained.

Little did I know that in a few moments I would be called to help with two emergencies that would change, forever, some of my perspective. Listening closely, I learned a lot. Every event and occasion gave me insight into the culture. Most of the patients were children with various needs, especially for immunizations: whooping cough, measles, polio. Others needed minor treatments, such as a bandage applied to a wound. Mothers carrying their infants seemed at ease in this, their Indian hospital; here they spoke their language and wore their native dress. They seemed relaxed and at home in the clinic.

Kicked in the Belly

Suddenly one of the nurses I had met the day before came running into the clinic, "Quick, Doña Blanca! [Since I just arrived yesterday,

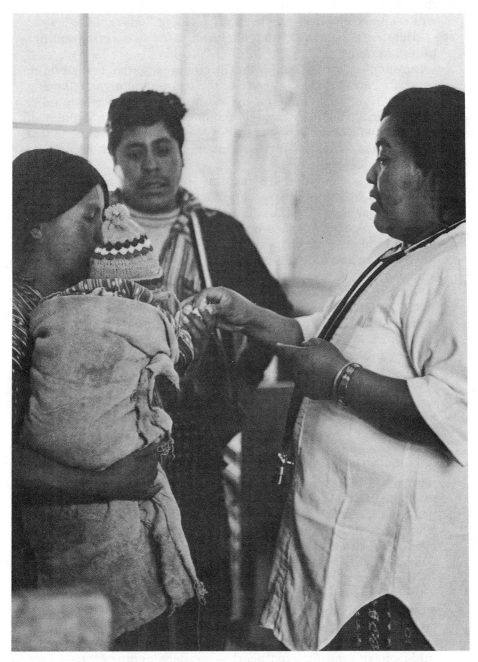

Magdelena, a woman committed to improving the lives of the Mayan peoples

they didn't know my name as yet, so they called me a "generic" white—Blanca.] There has been an accident," she shouted.

"Help, help, help! Edith can't help; she's too sick," cried another Indian nurse.

Running without asking what the emergency was, I crossed the courtyard and hurried into one of the examining areas following the Indian nurses. There, on the examining table, was a bundle, wrapped in a poncho. At one end I could see the face of a frightened, wrinkled old woman—maybe seventy years old—whose pain-filled eyes seemed to ask for mercy. I instinctively opened the poncho and nearly gasped aloud.

"My god! Look at all those intestines hanging out and the blood all over her belly and the poncho. What do I do now? Help! Oh my god!" I pleaded. What did I remember from Gray's *Human Anatomy*? Seconds flashed by. I couldn't remember anything. Or maybe I did. Yes, yes, it was coming back. Keep the area moist. Keep it clean and moist. What could have happened? Maybe it was a machete fight, or maybe her family was trying to do her in—no, no they're here, I guess that's her son, the one hugging her arm. What do I do? I couldn't yell in Spanish, just in English. Who would understand me? Help, help! Thoughts raced in fragments through my brain. Now memories of the long days in the operating room as a beginning nursing student assisting the surgeon with Kelly clamps and sutures seemed to be coming back into my mind.

What should I do? Checking her pulse, I found it unsurprisingly weak and rapid. My Nightingale Pledge kept flashing in my mind; I had promised to never do harm. But then again, this poor, old woman might go into shock and die—hurry! I began using sign language. I motioned to the small Indian nurse who was beside me to help me lift the end of the table onto blocks of wood that were lying in the corner of the room. With that loss of blood the patient might be in shock, and raising the end of the table would help keep her blood pressure somewhat elevated and, I hoped, prevent her from going further into shock and dying. Then we grabbed some clean sheets from a shelf nearby and threw them over the trembling woman, trying to keep her warm.

"Keep her warm," I said, out loud, in English—to the wind.

"Where are the sutures, a place to 'scrub,' saline solution for the wound, sulfa powder, what else . . . what do I need? Novocaine . . . do they have novocaine?" I spoke to myself. The fragile woman seemed to be bearing up under the emergency; I was glad. Another middle-aged man hovered nearby—perhaps another son—I gave him eye contact and tried to assure him that we were coping. My newly acquired assistant remained by my side. We hurriedly assembled a tray of instruments that I found wrapped in a clean towel on a shelf—some novocaine for suturing, a package of needles, and catgut sutures. That's all I'll need, I thought.

Just then a tall, blonde, husky man came rushing in. "I'm Mike, a Peace Corps volunteer. I heard that you were here. Doc says that you are to suture her up, but sprinkle the sulfa powder in before you begin. It's on the shelf by the sink. He's in the middle of another emergency, and John McCory won't be back for three days; he had to go into San Miguel—some fellow lost his leg in a car accident. I can help you with the Spanish if you need me."

Without realizing it, I began giving orders in English. We worked together—Mike, the Indian nurse, and I. I felt as if I had done this work many times before, as if I had held these needles, clamps, and sutures in my hands all my life. I hadn't, but I had assisted surgeons in the operating room as a student nurse. So, somewhere in my mind I held these memories. Under the stress these bits of information seemed to be as clear as the day I first learned them.

Quickly I scrubbed my hands in the sink and put on some latex gloves that probably were not sterile, but somehow I knew that some protection was better than using my bare hands. I picked up a syringe and loaded it with novocaine; then I began deadening the area around the wound with injections of the anesthetic. Next I took the hemostat and placed the semi-circular needle with catgut suturing thread in it, holding it firmly in my grip. Then I began to stitch.

Keep the stitches small, I told myself, use the deep muscle first, across and across, tie and cut. I prayed for no more bleeding. God, I thought, what if I puncture something? No, no, the blood looks like "old" blood. She's not bleeding anymore.

"Pour in more saline, Mike." It was my voice. I was doing this. Mike responded by following the orders. "Not too much, now. Sprinkle more of that sulfa powder right into the wound," I ordered, again.

"I think I'm going to vomit," Mike wailed, turning ashen.

"No, you're not. Just breathe deeply, keep breathing through your mouth. Just think of it as part of a movie and you're in the audience. Keep cool." I spoke calmly to him, meanwhile telling myself, Keep stitching, tie knots, cut. . . . Keep stitching. . . . All of the intestines are in now, and the hole is smaller and smaller.

"No, I'm really going to faint," Mike moaned again.

"No, just keep cool, cool, cool," I droned.

"What happened to her anyway?" I asked, beginning to focus on the whole situation and not just the stitching.

"Her son says she was kicked in the belly by a cow," Mike said weakly, color in his face returning.

"I guess that could happen," I acknowledged, thinking that until now I hadn't known that Indians kept cows.

"It must really hurt, but she's not crying. Why not?" I asked in a puzzled way. Mike answered, "These people are really tough. I've never seen one cry."

I looked at the incision, which I had closed with catgut and lots of sweat. The job was done; the stitches looked strangely even. I dabbed some Merthiolate on the wound and then took off the latex gloves and washed my hands again. Mike looked strong and calm again. We asked two men, perhaps her sons, to help us carry the wounded woman to one of the beds in the hospital.

"Keep her back straight," I cautiously reminded them. The old woman was laid down on a narrow bed without any bedding. The sons stayed close by. A couple of nurses came to her side and began talking with her in Cakchiquel and put a blanket over her. Moments later Doc entered, looking tired and haggard; he looked at the wound and the suturing.

"You did fine," was his only comment. "Let her eat only a little soup for a couple days and some Incaparina [a protein drink specially made in Guatemala by the Instituto Nutrición Centro América y Panamá]." Doc left quickly. A week later when I had returned from Xajáxac, I found the old woman walking about the courtyard; her bowels were working, and within another week she and her sons went on the bus to their home a remote twenty kilometers away. People went about their business as if this were a daily occurrence; it hadn't been for me. Some things you do because you have to.

Mike and I, exhausted, went across the street to the tienda for a cup of coffee, a sweet roll, and time to get acquainted. "I can't thank you enough, Mike, for coming in and helping me. What do you do around here?" I asked.

"I'm one of the Peace Corps volunteers like John. I have been here eight months helping the Indians to write up bylaws and such for their cooperatives. I was studying law in the United States and just needed to take a break from some of that lifestyle," he answered directly.

"Has it been all that you thought it might be—joining the Peace Corps?" I asked.

"I'll never be the same person, for sure," Mike continued. "There is so much poverty, ignorance, and prejudice here. Some days I think there is no hope, and then I see how strong the people are. Like today, when those sons carried their mother for over twenty

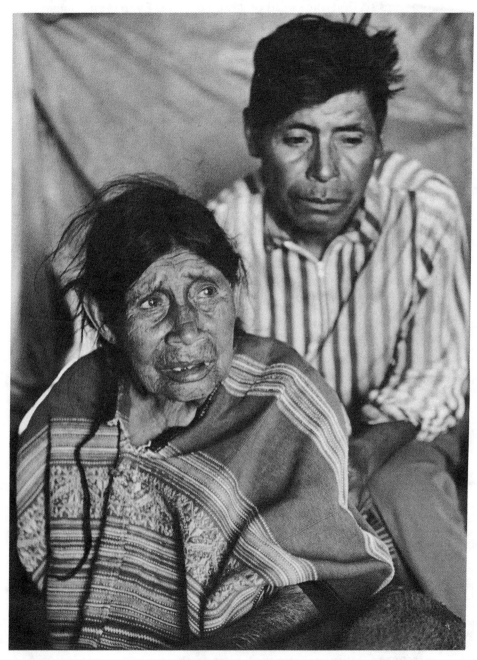

Mayan mother and son—illness is a shared experience

kilometers so that she could be taken care of. Even if she doesn't make it, I know we're pulling together, and things can change."

Baby Rosa in My Arms

We had just finished drinking our coffee and eating the sweet roll, when a man running into the tienda came to our table, speaking very fast in Spanish. Mike looked sad. "What's he saying?" I asked, as I couldn't understand his rapid speech.

"He said that Doc wants you to come right back, fast, because a very sick baby has just been brought in from one of the villages," Mike cried out. He threw some money on the table, and I joined him in a fast run across the road, back into the hospital, across the patio, and into the same room where we had helped the old woman.

Just then Doc came running in, holding a small baby in his arms. "Help her," he said to me. "Give her oxygen, get her to breathe. I don't know if she'll make it . . . she's so malnourished." His eyes seemed filled with the pain of having seen too many babies lost. He put the small bundle into my arms, saying as he turned to run back to the clinic, "We have five emergencies right now. Do what you can." Later, much later, I would reflect on what it means in developing countries not to have enough health care providers—now I needed to deal with the moment.

As I looked at her, I thought, How small she is, a soft bundle dressed in pink. Yet of her eyes, only the whites showed, and they were fixated. She lay with her head thrown back, limp and barely breathing. I knew she was nearly gone. Oxygen, he'd said, give her oxygen.

Where was the oxygen? Oh, yes, there's a tank and a sort-of-tent of plastic. I hurried through the motions.

My hands were stiff as I tried to set up the makeshift oxygen tent. Now the baby, I thought, Oh, she is so limp, but she's breathing. Barely.

I placed the limp little form on the table with some sheets underneath, motioning for the mother and Mike to help me. We were all alone, just Mike, the mother, and I. I knew she was the baby's mother—you could tell by her eyes. She, the mother, watched every move I made.

"What is her name?" I asked, in Spanish.

"Rosa," came the soft answer.

"Help me, Mike, get the tank over to the table," I ordered. We worked fast, as Rosa's little face was still motionless, her color growing dusky, the breathing hardly detectable. We placed the plastic tent over the baby and around the sheets on the table and started the oxygen going; I tried to make a tight shield of the tent so that the oxygen couldn't escape. Somewhere in this makeshift emergency room I recalled the rows and rows of children with polio whom we had cared for in the 1950s when I was still a student nurse. We had so many in oxygen tents then, too, and so many died. Some things don't change—like children dying.

With the makeshift oxygen tent in place, I gently massaged Rosa's chest and lifted the frail arms. A gasp, a cry! Had I heard right?

"Look!" cried Mike. "Look! She's opening her eyes!"

Little Rosa's eyes began to focus. She saw me and now began crying harder, and, wonderfully, harder. Her dusky face turned pinkish and then ruddy; Rosa's arms flailed about reaching outward. The mother, by my side, began to cry . . . and so did Mike and I. The room suddenly became still, like a cathedral.

I had not noticed, but about twenty Cakchiquel Indians had quietly entered the room; they were watching intently. In a moment, all of them got down on their knees. They were praying. The whole room was full of praying Indians. Some moved closer to me and Mike and began to touch the hem of my uniform.

"Santa Blanca, Santa Blanca," I heard them mumbling.

"No, it can't be," I said with astonishment to Mike, "Do they think they are witnessing a miracle? They must think I am a saint!"

"Yeah. They really do," said Mike with disbelief.

We were all quiet.

Little Rosa cried robustly; the sound shook the space. The mother, sobbing, pleaded to hold her little daughter.

"Please let me hold her; she is so hungry. I have milk. Please let me hold her. She seems so strong, why not?" the mother begged.

"Wait a while," I said, as gently as I knew how. The stronger the lusty cry became, the more the mother begged to hold and breastfeed Baby Rosa. I could feel the tension: a mother's love, an infant's need, the reaching out. I thought, "I guess it's okay." Gently, I took little Rosa out from under the makeshift oxygen tent and placed her next to her mother's breast.

Gasping, I saw the problem—the mother's abscessed breasts, the crusted nipples, her emaciated body. She herself was a skeleton—a starving being. How could she have any breastmilk? But the mother's cooing sounds seemed like music; it filled the quiet room as mother and baby became one. Eager sucking sounds came from Baby Rosa but then, in only a few minutes, slowly—almost as if in a slow motion movie—I couldn't believe it: I watched as the grasp of Rosa's little hand loosened on her mother's breast; her rosy cheeks turned an ashen gray. Her body went limp as a rag doll. Rosa was gone—dead in her mother's arms, as were her other six brothers and sisters who never lived to see their first birthday. All of them gone, in just a few years. I could do nothing. Rosa's mother was sobbing, knowingly; the comfort of her abscessed, empty breasts was to have been little Rosa's last memory. Perhaps it was best; I wished I knew.

I turned off the oxygen tent; big Mike hugged me and then the mother; we all hugged. The Indians filed quietly out, into the courtyard and beyond—returning, I supposed, to their empty fields. As the lilies in the fields . . . so the winds passeth . . . knowing the place no more, I thought as I struggled not to cry but to maintain control. I can't stand all of this death, I thought. I walked out into the woods behind the hospital, leaned against a sturdy tree, and sobbed.

"How can it be?" I asked the sky. "Isn't this just a perpetuation of death?" Empty breasts and empty fields—where does it end? How about my own well-nourished children so far away? Oh, how I missed them! I wished I were home. About then I heard a noise behind me, and I looked back and saw Doc. He came over to me and put his hand on my shoulder and said, "I know it hurts; it never stops hurting, but you did what you could. We can never save them. They don't have enough antibodies to fight the infections. And we don't have the right kind of Band-Aid to fight the poverty. The people need land to fight their hunger." I was to learn many more lessons about poverty in the years to come, but the lesson of Baby Rosa will always be a painful part of me, and that pain has brought a curious strength and courage. I had much more to learn from these people of the mountains. It was almost noon; the morning had been long, and Magdelena and I still had to do our shopping for the next morning's trip into the remote mountains.

Chapter 4

A Penny Capital System

We value life and we see death as a distinct part of life. The opposite of death is not life but birth. When death comes, we think of the corn. We feel the grain and know that it is alive. We put it in the ground where it is born again as a plant.
—Maria Hortensia Otzoy de Cap, in *A New Dawn in Guatemala*, Richard Luecke, ed., 1993

I hurried to the clinic, where I found Magdelena waiting for me. Greeting me with a big smile, she said, nonchalantly, "I hear you had a busy morning."

"Yes, I really have; I've really learned a lot," I replied. I wanted to talk more, to share my sorrow, but lacking the right Spanish words and then not knowing how people here responded to death, I said nothing. But I watched for Magdelena's response.

"I guess we never really get used to losing a baby, but you know that over half the children born here in the highlands die before they are five years old. We cry and then go on with life," Magdelena responded, and then changed the subject.

An Indigenous Market

"Now I'll show you how we shop in Chimaltenango. We don't have any McDonald's here!" she laughed. What they did have were mounds of fresh fruits and vegetables, herbs, live poultry, and newly butchered beef. The indigenous population came, in droves, three times a week—Tuesdays, Fridays, and Sundays—from a more-than-

41

fifty kilometer area surrounding Chimaltenango. They walked (barefoot, mostly) over the rugged, winding trails, carrying their home-grown produce and products (chickens, pigs, fruits and vegetables, blankets and weavings, so many things) on their backs or heads. Or, after walking from the footpaths of their local fields and homes to a highway, they would climb aboard one of several types of "chicken buses," as they are called, to travel to the market center.

This market system has been the major economic exchange system in the highlands since before the Spanish Conquest. The structure of the system remains the same: the local produce and products are exchanged for cash and sometimes barter, in order for the hoe-and-machete independent farmers to buy the supplies that the family needs. A family will use the small margin of profit to purchase either seed grain for the next harvest or some luxury, such as a comb, a cooking or eating utensil, or skeins of wool or cotton for weaving into clothing for the family (sometimes they will embroider the articles of clothing and sell them to tourists). I could quickly see that the market center represents a subsistence system, because the level of profit is so slight. The margin for error is very small; poor health or the death of one member of the family or a devastating natural disaster (floods, volcanoes, drought, damaging winds, earthquakes—all are possible here) can destroy an entire household. A family depends upon the productivity of each member. All elderly people and children are expected to contribute to the family economy. (However, I did find that infanticide is practiced when a child is born with multiple defects, and "miracles" are not performed on severely ill elderly people as they are in the United States medical care system.) Furthermore, since there is no crop insurance and since the federal government does not declare national emergencies, a family also depends upon the conditions of the environment for its welfare. The peasant market economy, which is subject to the larger national economy, is a fragile system; therefore, nothing in this society is wasted. Nothing is discarded. Recycling is part of the texture of the system and is not a trend, but a means of survival.

Family as an Economic Unit

Both men and women are agriculturalists and entrepreneurs; men cultivate corn, and women grow vegetables, fruits, and flowers. Women also weave cloth and decorative products; men do some sewing in some areas, but they are not the weavers. Men carry the heaviest cargo to the market; the women carry the weavings and flowers, their own food supply, and, of course, the children. A woman securely supports her youngest infant on her back in a *rebozo*, a handwoven, shawl-like covering, made from heavy woolen or cotton material. The infant's head is usually covered with a knitted cap for warmth—and also to keep the evil spirits from entering the child. However, in spite of being nearly covered, one can easily tell the gender of the infant by catching a glimpse of the child's earlobes, as infant girls have pierced ears, almost at birth, and wear tiny beaded earrings. Babies are dressed in the same, native wraparound cloth, without diapers, until about the age of three, at which time boys wear trousers and shirts, mostly handwoven, and girls wear traditional wraparound skirts with matching tops.

As I watched the parades of Indian families, I noticed they seemed to move in unity; when watching them on the trails or in the streets, I found it was like seeing a small pyramid in motion. The mother and father were in the middle, the peak, with children, usually four, two on each side, each touching the other. Each family carried their own food: tortillas wrapped in cloth and small earthenware jars of cooked, mashed black beans. Some members carried small tin containers of cooked rice, and others had coffee or a chocolate drink. They were a self-contained, self-sufficient economic unit.

Why all this discussion about the way an Indian family walks? I believe that by analyzing variation in the microbehaviors of people, we grow to comprehend variation in social relationships and thus understand different cultures. Adams (1970) points out that a study of a culture should make the connections between cultural forms and social behavior. I believe that the way an Indian family interacts is the foundation for its cultural form. The Indian family is a cooperative, microunit of the peasant economy. The regional market system is the economic outlet for their household produce.

The street on which I walked every morning and evening to and from the pension was, on this market day, packed with people, from one side to the other, for at least three or four blocks. Sellers and buyers filled every inch of space. Each "penny capitalist" was calling out loudly, bargaining seriously, in competition with all the other vendors. (Prices rose or dropped depending on the availability of the produce and the number of customers and so was what Sol Tax (1953) called a penny capitalist system.) Vegetables and fruits were sold in areas that were clearly defined by plastic or hand-woven mats placed on the ground. Most of these self-declared "stores" were covered with a temporary shelter fashioned from some kind of awning material, usually plastic, hung over a wooden

Penny capitalism, a competitive market scene

frame. This shelter protected the merchants from the direct near-equator sun and the monsoonal rains, but the shelter also defined a boundary space. The sellers and the buyers alike knew their business. The sellers were cunning to the penny, keeping their prices competitive with all others in the area and adjusting as the number of customers waxed and waned. In season, fruits and vegetables were abundant—and a bargain, by their standards—but out of season, the prices shifted. Buyers knew just how far they could haggle for the best bargain without insulting the seller. Sellers, too, kept their margin of profit at the lowest level.

Marketing As Social Exchange

We threaded ourselves through the mass of competition and price wrangling, Magdelena, with her broad girth, leading the way. People along the way greeted her and stared at me, a tall, blonde gringa. When we approached our first vendor, Magdelena's smiling face became deadly serious, as she began to bargain the price down to half—never insulting the seller, but letting even the strongest merchant know that she was not to be cheated. Walking farther along the trail of vendors, we entered a long shed filled with more merchants and buyers. Here we found a different class of merchant, the permanent sellers, and aisles of tables and bins filled with less perishable goods: beans, rice, dried herbs, fish, butchered poultry, and huge slabs of beef. Also in this building were stalls where nonlocal merchandise was sold—a whole department store of goods: needles, thread, combs, lightweight metal cooking utensils, gaudy plastic plates, pitchers, bowls, poorly constructed underwear, barrettes, ribbons, yard goods, plastic shoes, and simple cotton-polyester shirts and trousers. The merchants of these goods are usually Ladinos, who buy the products in Guatemala City and transport them to the highlands. Most of the nonlocal products are manufactured in Central American countries, and the prices are fixed, meaning that a buyer cannot bargain for a lower price.

The sounds and smells of market day are unforgettable. I had learned from John on our first trip from the airport that one can identify the village or area from which people come by the color and design of their shirts, blouses, skirts, and even their trousers. On an ordinary day in one of the villages, all the colors are the same, but on market day, a town is a rainbow of color, filled with people from many different villages. Reds, blues, and yellows are the most popular colors. While I preferred seeing the beautiful native clothes, some local people said the Western-style Ladino clothes are less expensive than Indian woven clothes. On the other hand, many also said that the Western-style dress, often of polyester, is not as comfortable as is the traditional heavy cotton or wool clothing. Magdelena mentioned that the cloth jackets bought in Guatemala City don't keep out the cold and the rain of the high altitude as well as the woolen ones made in Chimaltenango. "You'll see what I mean when we get to Xajáxac," she laughed. I thought about my polyester blue-and-white-striped uniform dress and the white polyester sweater I had brought to wear at the outlying clinic and wondered if I had packed senselessly. I learned very quickly on that first trip to Xajáxac that I should have brought a wool sweater—I nearly froze to death!

Even though the native clothing is ecologically more adaptive, for the women, at least, Western-style clothing is often more practical. For instance, it takes a woman two to three weeks of weaving four to five hours a day with a backstrap loom (a type of loom that requires that the weaver sit on the ground facing the frame, which is drawn tightly and tied behind her back with a strap)

Indian women resting on market day—the market is also a place for gossiping and courting a mate

to weave the cloth with which to make her *traje*, or clothing. A Western-style outfit can easily be purchased for cash from one of the local merchants. One can quickly see that such a shift in cultural norms and behaviors involves a shift in other norms and behaviors relating to men's and women's work roles and statuses in the household. These shifts or cultural changes put into motion a rippling series of adjustments.

Market day is a time to make money, but it is also a time to exchange information, to see relatives, to gossip, and to have fun. For those who are single, market day might also be the day to look for a mate. On most market days I would see one or two "traveling medicine men" (in my encounters they were always male), otherwise known as con-artists. First the salesman would lay out his wares, bottles of various colored liquids with or without labels. He would also display pamphlets illustrating official-looking miracles. Usually the pamphlets showed a frail-looking young man (no pamphlets showed the miracle effects upon women) taking the liquid. In the next pictures he had turned into a very virile, energized hunk of man, grinning from ear to ear. The text of the pamphlet was not nearly as inspiring, as it described the various ailments the elixir would treat: worms, loss of kidney control, constipation, and the like. But the words that were intended to catch readers' attention were "increased sexual virility," prominently underlined. One could hear about these so-called miracles over the market traffic, as the salesman proclaimed, sometimes with a megaphone or microphone, all the wonders of his latest finds. There was usually brisk business at his table. Magdelena disgustedly declared, "He is just a thief of the people's money."

On occasion, I would see a game of chance, usually a variation of the "shell game," but overall the market days were business days. I didn't often see drunkenness, except on Sunday markets, and then usually after the market closed at sundown.

Some people also visit the town's cathedral on market day, where they confess their sins, light candles, or pray. The majority of Indians and Ladinos in Guatemala are members of the Catholic church. In the more remote villages, the Catholic church is less traditional than in the larger towns and retains residuals of earlier indigenous beliefs and practices. Referred to as "folk catholicism," an indigenous priest or the local people carry out a mixture of Christian and ancient rituals, with vestiges of ancestor worship and perhaps worship of other gods.

Soon our market basket was full; Magdelena had picked out potatoes, carrots, squash, onions, tomatoes, papaya, and pineapple. We had no meat or milk. "Tomorrow, before we leave, we'll buy our bread, fresh from the baker, and we'll buy our tortillas from a neighbor when we get to Xajáxac. All you need to bring is your sweater and a poncho in case of rain; the rainy season is about to start," Magdelena explained as she looked up at the cloudless sky.

"I'll see you at eight in the morning in the plaza," I called to her as we went our separate ways. I trudged home, exhausted, thinking that shopping at the native market, although exciting and new, took all my energy. A growing awareness crept over me that the energy expended at McDonald's was someone else's or a machine's—not mine. That had been one of those principles I'd learned in a course on economic anthropology; industrialization involves a shift in energy use from the human to the machine. After reminding myself that I was now living in a nonindustrialized society, I fell soundly asleep.

Chapter 5

Xajáxac
Black Waters and Witch Doctors

> To ask me to verify my life by giving you my statistics, said
> Casteneda, is like using science to validate sorcery. It robs the
> world of its magic.
> —Carlos Casteneda, *The Teachings of Don Juan*, 1968

Little did I know that my world was again about to change. How
can I explain what it is like to enter a place that, as far as I could
see, had hardly changed for over four hundred years? Perhaps in
anticipation, I ate more heartily that morning, not knowing when
I would eat again. I explained to the young man at La Bohemia,
who could now understand me, that I would not be back for several
days and that I was going to work in a hamlet called Xajáxac. He
replied, "I've never heard of that place." His remark gave me the
shudders.

I walked quickly to the plaza, arriving with about ten minutes
to spare, yet there was Magdelena already waiting, looking fresh
and excited. "I like Xajáxac more than anyplace else in the world,"
she said laughing. "I hope you do, too."

A Chicken Bus to Heaven

Soon we boarded a dilapidated bus called the Blue Bird, along
with forty or fifty other travelers as well as chickens, pigs, and loads
of produce and purchases. There wasn't room for all of us! But we

squeezed, grunted, pushed until all the people and produce were in or somewhere on top of the bus. I soon realized that I was not really sitting on a seat but was merely suspended, midair, between the hipbones of two other people. All manner of human behavior had to take place in this bus. Children urinated, old men coughed, some vomited. But all cared for one another. For example, at one point while going around a curve, a live rooster fell from the shelf above our seats and landed on top of one man's head. Everyone began to laugh and then tried to capture the frightened, escaped rooster.

We swayed and turned together as one long chain, as the bus climbed higher and higher into the mountains, an old veteran swerving around sharp corners. I stared straight ahead as we careened near the edge of a steep *barranca* (ravine) with over 4,000 feet to the bottom. I stole a glance at Magdelena. She was relaxed—in fact, sleeping. I naively trusted the driver, who seemed unconcerned with the responsibility he had. He was laughing and trying to flirt with the young woman in the seat behind him. Later in my work I was to see fragile highways and bridges disappear into the deep ravines under the onslaught of the heavy monsoon rains. I also learned that the tall pine trees lining the road have very shallow roots and act as no barrier; they topple like match sticks if a heavy bus hits them as it rounds one of the sharp curves, thus taking the busload of passengers and produce into their flight down the steep slopes of these volcanic mountains. Routine travel in developing countries can be very dangerous, not the fun-filled, luxury tours we fantasize about in the United States.

Midway to Xajáxac the bus stopped for a break: everyone scurried out, running to the restaurant called Katok (in Cakchiquel this means "come in"; it was also Magdelena's last name), which was also a *palapa* (structure with a thatched roof). Many vendors on the side of the road yelled loudly, trying to compete with the restaurant in selling their hot tortillas and cool drinks. Magdelena and I hurried into Katok, where we found tasty sandwiches, drinks, and sweets. I watched what Magdelena ate and then had the same thing. We hurried to the bathroom, where we waited in long lines. Then, with the sound of the horn, Magdelena said, "It's time to go back."

We hurried back into the tight cocoon of a chicken bus to finish our four-hour journey. After about two more hours of the swirling ride, Magdelena said, "This is where we will get off. We have a few more miles to go, and then we have to catch a little bus to Xajáxac."

The driver stopped the bus. We negotiated our way out of the crowd and then stood by the side of the road for about fifteen minutes. Soon a small van with only three seats stopped for us; I noticed the driver had to pump the brakes for every curve as we wound our way through steep cliffs. Suddenly, Magdelena yelled, "*Aquí, no más!*" (Here, no more!) We had arrived in Xajáxac.

Patterns of Household Living

It didn't look like much of anything to me: one little shed, a longer shed, a volleyball net, a small adobe tienda, and an outhouse—that was about all there was to see. But I wasn't surprised, as Magdelena had described Xajáxac to me as we traveled. "Some people think Xajáxac means 'step by step'; others think it means 'black water,'" she began. "Of the 2,020 people who live there, eleven are Ladino, a clear minority! The rest are Cakchiquel Mayan Indians," she explained. "In the dry season the rivers are very small, with black water, but in the rainy season these rivers can become large and swift. Most of the houses scattered about have adobe walls, tile roofs, and earthen floors. Huts of the poorer folk are made from cane and have thatched roofs. Each house is one room with a *corredor* [open porch] in front. There are no glass windows, but rather each house has an open window with a hinged covering for protection against the rain and wind—and, of course, a front door."

Magdelena continued, "Inside are mats on which people sleep and occasionally hammocks for children. An open fire—made by igniting dry wood sticks, gathered daily from the fields and distant areas—is used for cooking. The people are finding it harder and harder to find enough wood for cooking each day, because they have cut down most of the trees to plant more corn. (Notice how the lower branches of the trees are stripped for firewood, but the tree is still alive.) Inside is a metal sheet suspended on rocks, cement blocks or old tin cans for cooking. In ancient times the rocks used for cooking were considered sacred, as Cakchiquels believe the hearth is the soul of the home, a special place. A mother is called *alma de la casa*, or soul of the house—sort of the same thing. Corn and other food supplies, such as salt, are stored in earthen jars (although nowadays you can find many plastic ones, too). Earthen jars are made here in the highlands.

"Each person has only two outfits, and maybe a special blouse or jacket for ceremonies and celebrations; they don't need closets like you do in the United States. They just hang their clothes on nails and wash them in the stream by pounding and rubbing with a homemade *jabon* [soap]. They dry their clothes by laying them out on the grass near the house to catch the intense sunrays."

Grandmother, with grandchild, and mother prepare a meal together

I sensed that Magdelena enjoyed teaching me about their ways, and as we traveled, I asked lots of questions, such as, "What's it like to be a woman here?"

Magdelena answered, "Women do the housekeeping and cooking and of course have children and raise them. Corn, raised in their adjacent fields, is the major supply of food. Each day women spend almost two hours grinding the corn with the *mano* and *metate* (similar to a rolling pin and a tray), which were also used by the ancient Maya. In the larger villages, a businessperson (not always a man) may have a gasoline-powered or electric corn grinder. This is a tremendous convenience, because it frees a woman from more than half her corn-grinding time to attend to the other needs of the family. Girls learn to do the corn grinding by the age of eight.

"People eat beans, rice, and tortillas every day. Tortillas are made by placing a ball of ground corn mash, *masa*, in the palm of your hands and patting it into a circle." (She demonstrated with her hands.) "Lime in water is used to soak and soften the kernels of corn for the mash," she said before pausing.

I had seen big chunks of the white compound in the market but didn't know it was lime. "I have heard that some doctors think that softening the corn with lime (or I believe it is a type of lye) is hard on the teeth, and they suspect it causes gallstones.''

"I wouldn't be surprised," Magdelena replied. "We have a lot of problems with tooth decay and also with gall bladder attacks.''

She continued, "Life for a woman in the highlands is hard. She plants corn for the family near the home, not to sell, but to eat. In the early morning she prepares meals for the male members of the family to take with them to the fields—they leave at about 4:00 A.M. A woman searches for firewood, fetches water from the stream, washes the clothes, tends the small livestock (such as goats, sheep, and poultry), and weaves many yards of cloth for making blouses, *faldas* [skirts], *pantolones* [trousers], *camisas* [shirts], shawls, rebozos, and *cinchos* [belts]. It's a hard life for both men and women," Magdelena concluded by waving her hands in the air, as if to plead for help.

"I would guess it has good parts, too," I quickly added. "Tell me about the marriage practices.''

"That is very interesting," Magdelena blossomed again. "In the small hamlets, there is usually no marriage ceremony when a couple decides to marry; people just say they are married by consent. After several years a travelling priest may perform a marriage ceremony, but it's not required here in the highlands.

"The couple—usually the boy is about seventeen or eighteen years and the girl is fifteen or sixteen years old—will have met at several places, such as at a stream or the school, and have talked. There's no dating as in the United States; there is no formal courting. It is the girl's parents who will ask for a marriage or an 'arrangement.' Sometimes the boy's family will give a chicken or rooster to the girl's family, but they don't exchange much; people here in Xajáxac have so little that they can't exchange.''

"Where does the new couple live, alone or with his family?" I asked inquisitively.

"Most of the time it's the girl who moves into the boy's parents' home; she then does household chores like all the others in that house. But after the birth of their first child, the new husband and wife will build their own home, often within the same compound as the boy's parents," answered Magdelena. I knew that she had just described a patrilineal kinship system and a patrilocal, and then neolocal, residential system. This means the inheritance pattern follows the male line, and with the birth of the first child, a couple establishes a new household by living in a separate house.

"Tell me something about the men in this village. What do they do?" I asked.

"It's the males in a Cakchiquel family who till the fields. At about

Author Glittenberg with Indian sales"men"

age eight, a boy begins working in the fields alongside his father, brothers, and uncles. He is first trained to use a small hoe to clear the fields of weeds and to assist in harvesting the corn (which is planted annually) and beans. As he grows in strength, a young man is expected to work in the fields almost every day except on Sunday. Using a large metal hoe with a blade about fifteen inches across, he will dig drainage ditches that are about two or three feet deep. (We'll walk in them tomorrow, so that you can see how deep they are.) The only place available for planting corn is on these perpendicular hillsides. You can imagine what a problem that is when the rains come; they almost wipe away the soil. Some men have to walk two hours to reach their fields. As the family grows, they have less and less land to plant, so they have to go farther and farther away to find empty land—land that they can buy or rent. The best land, the flat land, belongs to the finca owners. They plant coffee there and sell it for export." Magdelena described this situation matter-of-factly.

She continued, "About midmorning the men usually stop to have a drink of water, coffee, or a rice mixture called *atole*. At midday they eat tortillas and beans, and they have the same meal again at night. When the sun sets, the men return home. At night the whole family sleeps together in one room on mats covered with ponchos—not like you do in the United States," she laughed. "All of you sleep in separate rooms and separate beds. So lonely," she laughed again. I knew that some day I would see whether this really was so or whether Magdelena just told me these things to fill the time or to amuse me. Yet I believed her. I knew I was learning about the patterns of living, the lifeways of the people, and that is what an anthropologist does.

"Do you think it's a good life here?" I asked.

"It's good, but not long; we don't live to be what you think of as old people," she answered. "The average lifespan for a man is only about fifty or so years, and for a woman it's shorter; usually a woman lives only about forty-five years. I'm told women die earlier here than in other places," she concluded.

"I think you're right; in the United States we live to be in our mid-seventies or eighties," I commented.

"That's *old!*" she gasped.

The Clinic in the Clouds

Having arrived safely at our destination, we walked up to a long adobe building. I could see about a dozen Indians lined up outside the clinic. On the other side of the compound was a similar building, only much bigger; this was the public school for children six to fourteen years old. Supposedly 150 children were enrolled, but during the time I was there, I never saw more than forty children attending classes at one time.

We entered the clinic. It consisted of a small examining room with a table, a scale, and five shelves containing medications kept in clear bottles. On one wall hung a stethoscope and a sphygmomanometer (for blood pressure measurement). On the other side of this wall were our living quarters: two beds, a table and two chairs, a small two-burner gas tabletop stove, and shelves for supplies. Next to this room was a large, empty room with several wooden chairs lined along a wall.

"This is the town hall, where the mayor and councilmen meet. It is also a room where we have families spend the night when one member is too sick to return home," Magdelena explained.

Next Magdelena brought out a large cardboard box that contained patient charts in envelopes, all in alphabetical order. She began putting a white smock over her colorful traje, and so I also put one over my polyester, blue-and-white-striped uniform. We were ready to see the first patient.

Together we saw each patient. Magdelena listened as the patient explained the ailment to her in Cakchiquel. I could not understand a single word, but their Mayan language sounded beautiful. I wished I could understand! Maybe in time . . . Magdelena would interpret everything for me in Spanish, and then I would examine the patient. We worked well together. I found that the problems were not severe: a man with malaria needed quinine; a child with diarrhea needed an antibiotic; a woman needed an injection for birth control; a woman with a large goiter needed to go to Chimaltenango for more tests and treatment. Magdelena followed up by talking with the patients about their health—counseling and teaching each one. I was impressed. I could tell these people trusted Magdelena; she treated them professionally and with kindness.

Two hours later we were alone. "Let's have some coffee," Magdelena suggested. I was so hungry, I was hoping she had intended we have something to eat too. We started the little gas stove and boiled some water. At 9,000 feet above sea level, it was cold and windy in our clinic in the clouds; I wished I had brought warmer clothes—and a *wool* sweater.

Soon, we had finished drinking our instant coffee and eating the bread we had bought from the baker before we left Chimaltenango. I was still hungry, but saw nothing else to eat. "Would you like to make the stew, for supper?" asked Magdelena.

"I would love to," I replied, thinking of the generous portions I would make. She left me to my work; I soon realized that *all* we had to eat was the food we had brought with us from Chimaltenango. There were neither stores, nor a market for additional shopping, so I measured the supplies very carefully to cover our meals for the next two days. Nothing was wasted.

As the stew cooked, it filled our little "home" with a savory smell. A few more patients came by, and soon the sun began to set. A neighbor brought us fresh tortillas and some apples. I noticed that she talked quietly with Magdelena; I couldn't eavesdrop, as they spoke in Cakchiquel. I listened and watched and noticed that something had disturbed Magdelena.

When it was time to eat, we sat at the small wooden table on still smaller chairs. If I could just get my knees under the table, I thought I would be comfortable, but my kneecaps protruded above the edge. Five-feet-nine isn't an ideal height when living with the Maya. As

Women waiting at the Xajáxac clinic

uncomfortable as the tiny chairs were, it beat sitting on the earthen
floor as the indigenous people did in their homes in Xajáxac. By
candlelight, Magdelena resembled a beautiful Buddha, but her
gentle smile and quiet ways were suddenly broken as she began
telling the unsettling news the neighbor had brought. "Thieves

entered one of the homes in a nearby hamlet, and they killed a man and his wife with machetes." Her Mayan eyes flashed a defiance I would never forget. She continued, "My parents were considered 'rich' Indians, for they worked hard and saved money to buy land. They were able to buy farms for each of us—for me and my two brothers," she spoke defensively. "But it hasn't been good." Magdelena's cheeks sagged, and her eyes filled with tears. "You see, two years ago my older brother was attacked by thieves. They used machetes; he fought hard, but they cut him deeply, and he died. Now his three children and wife have nothing but the land; she has no one to help her. She's like many in this area, a widow. It's like that nowadays," she concluded.

Magdelena's face turned fierce as she described the scenes. I no longer saw a Buddha, but a woman of conviction and valor. She went to the door and from behind it pulled a four-foot machete with an edge that glittered in the candlelight. Pulling herself up to her full five feet, she proclaimed, "I dare anyone to walk through the door."

I wondered how and when she would ever need to use it. I also wondered about my own strength and will. Having never been in combat or even in a small fistfight, would I survive? I thought then that perhaps my blonde hair and unusual height would frighten them away. Later I was to learn what I would really do to survive. And in the decade to pass, I was to learn more about many women of courage. Rebels (*los guerrilleros*), the army, and groups of thieves without any political connection would leave some villages without any men still living; these places have become known as the *aldeas de la viudas*, villages of widows. The confusion and devastation that the terrorism leaves behind paralyzes most people for a long time, some never recover.

We again became quiet as the winds groaned at the door. I said a prayer in English about my family far away, and Magdelena said one in Spanish that we would be kept safely through the night. We prepared our beds; I crawled inside my sleeping bag and wondered about the day and weeks ahead.

A Mysterious Picnic Brings a Sleepless Night

Morning burst upon us with the same suddenness as had the darkness of the night. In the precipitous mountains, the sun had no easy exit or appearance. I smelled coffee brewing and could hardly wait for yet another day. Breakfast was ample, with eggs fresh from our neighbor's chickens and hot tortillas from their grill (we didn't need a market or a store). The first patients began arriving early; there weren't many, so by midday we were in need of a break. "Let's go on a picnic," Magdelena suggested.

"Great," I replied, and began to gather bread, pineapple, and apples.

We carried our basket of food across a log bridge and up a small hill; as we neared the top, Magdelena said, "I'm taking you to the altar of the witch doctor." Some picnic, I thought, but I could hardly wait! As we approached the top of the hill, I could see a small open area a short distance ahead.

"See those two small wooden crosses at different angles and the bunches of flowers and fruits in front of each?" Magdelena asked.

"Yes, what is that?"

"That is an ancient Mayan custom," answered Magdelena, "There is a story about the two crosses and how they came to be found in the highlands of Guatemala. When the Spaniards first came to our land, their priests were very upset to see the Mayan people and their pagan worship. You see, the Maya already used a cross similar to the Christian cross in worshiping one of the Mayan gods. The Spanish priests said, 'Take down your pagan cross and put up the Christian cross.' This the Maya obediently did. However, in the years to follow, all types of problems troubled the natives: there were floods, earthquakes, and volcanic eruptions, everything. The troubled natives, wanting to stop the disasters, begged the priests, 'Please let us put our Mayan cross up again; we must be saved.' So the Spanish priests consented, and subsequently the volcanoes were quiet, and the floods were gone. Remember this story when you travel far away from the big city or other places. You will see that we, the indigenous people, put up not one cross, but two crosses—the Christian cross and the Mayan cross."

"That's interesting," I commented.

"I'm a Christian," Magdelena explained, "and I don't like the foolishness of the witch doctor's altar. I believe he is silly," she continued. "There are supposedly thirteen witches in this village of 2,020 people. The *brujo* [witch doctor] who has this altar is supposed to be the strongest of them all. But I don't believe in his black magic," she concluded defiantly. Magdelena threw garbage from our picnic onto the altar, as, I thought, a symbol of her defiance. My heart sank. I understood her disgust, but somehow an altar is a holy symbol to me, one to be respected even if one isn't a follower and believer of that faith. And so I was troubled. When we returned to our clinic we found only a few patients waiting, and we began to work as we had the day before.

The Witch Doctor's Dilemma

As evening approached, a tall man with a distinctive gait and posture entered the door. Suddenly Magdelena's face seemed more pale. She appeared surprised, or was it frightened? I was only beginning to read her moods.

"What is it that you need?" she asked professionally, in Cakchiquel.

"I have a wound on my leg that refuses to heal; I have had it for over a week now," the stately man answered in a deep voice.

"Please, pull up your pant leg," Magdelena requested. The wound on the leg was about six inches long; it was puffy around the cut and his entire leg was red. The small square of gauze dressing that had been placed on the wound was filled with yellow pus; it was badly infected.

"I think we should clean it with some hydrogen peroxide," I said, "and then put on some of the penicillin ointment." Magdelena nodded in agreement. I noticed that Magdelena didn't move toward the man, but let me change the bandage. I cleaned the wound carefully and put a thin line of penicillin ointment on the reddened gash.

"How did this happen?" I asked. The man talked softly in Cakchiquel, looking intently at Magdelena. As he prepared to leave, I gave the man some squares of gauze and the tube of penicillin and asked him to come to see us next week. He paid one quetzal and slowly left the clinic, disappearing into the field.

"How did that happen?" I asked Magdelena.

Magdelena's mouth seemed dry as she said, "Remember I told you about the witch doctor when we visited the altar today? Well, that man who just left the clinic was the head brujo of this area. It's his altar where we had the picnic today!" I remembered the garbage she had thrown on it. Her eyes looking frightened, she continued, "He says that another brujo is trying to take over the valley, and so put a curse into a dog; the dog came and bit this man, the head brujo. Since that time the wound does not seem to heal. He is afraid that there is more black magic going on."

"What do we do about that?" I asked innocently.

Magdelena shrugged her shoulders and continued looking worried. I thought the incident was strange, but not as strange as the events of the night that was to follow.

After supper that night, we washed the dishes and prepared for bed. Suddenly there was a howling just outside the door. Magdelena opened the door just a few inches and shouted, "Go away!" I saw a large, brown dog trying to come into the room. Magdelena grabbed a broom and tried to chase him away. She was unsuccessful; the dog stood his ground and began howling again at the front door.

I watched as Magdelena crossed her chest several times; I felt a chill in the air. "Is there some kind of danger?" I asked.

She didn't answer but instead went to the box of candles that was kept near the stove and took out a large white one. Magdelena lit the candle, got down on her knees, and began chanting in Cakchiquel; the tonal language seemed strangely powerful that night. A thin line of sweat appeared above her lip. I sat very, very quietly; I asked no questions. When she finished, she quietly blew out the flame. We both went silently to bed. Throughout the night I tried to sleep, but the dog continued to howl mournfully and persistently at our door. I don't believe either of us slept at all that night.

Morning again came too soon. After a night with no sleep the bright sunshine hurt my eyes. I had wanted to ask Magdelena questions, but something told me to keep quiet and observe. As the sun came up, the brown dog disappeared into the field. Magdelena told me that she was going to our neighbor's hut for the tortillas. She said that she would also look for some flowers. I watched as her sturdy figure crossed the log bridge and ambled up the hill to the witch doctor's altar. She was gone for almost an hour, and I began to wonder if she was ever coming back. Suddenly there she was, coming through the doorway—and looking tranquil again. I knew that, in her own way, she had made her peace with the spirits of the witch doctor. We never discussed the situation again, nor did we have another picnic at the altar.

After seeing a few more patients with common ailments, we packed our basket, locked the clinic door, and headed back to the lower lands of Chimaltenango. It was about noon as we walked up the hill to the main highway and found an overloaded chicken bus going to Chimaltenango. As we neared the city, the skies opened up. Lightning seemed to strike everything and everywhere. I knew the monsoonal season had begun. Each season has its blessings and its curses. This season would bring freshness to the stunted, wilted corn, and emaciated cattle would begin to fatten as the weeks went by. Roads would be hard to cross, however. People would be killed by falling rocks, boulders, and lightning. Some adobe houses on the street where I walked to the hospital would be weakened under the unrelenting rains, and their walls would melt into piles of mud, exposing the families who lived within.

During the weekly treks to Xajáxac, I grew to understand the strengths and weaknesses of the Cakchiquel. I discovered their rhythm of life was persistent, in spite of the struggles. The witch doctor came to see us each week. We soon learned that there were not thirteen brujos in the valley, as Magdelena had thought, but rather seventy-five. Our visitor was still considered the most powerful. "Another one is always trying to take my power," he explained to Magdelena.

In spite of our modern medicine, the brujo's wound did not heal during the six weeks we visited Xajáxac. He seemed to accept the penicillin's ineffectiveness. Feeling that he trusted us, I asked, "Would you mind if we visited your home?"

"Of course not, the brujo replied. "Come with me." The brujo led as Magdelena and I followed him across the log bridge, up a hill, and then across fields of lilies and corn and other vegetables. We arrived at last at a large square compound comprised of several buildings, only one of which was a house (as evidenced by the sacred corn hanging above the doorway and the open corredor so typical of the native houses).

The brujo led us into the house. As my eyes became accustomed to the dim light, I saw the usual arrangement of things: a large pot of stew was cooking on the fire, filling the room with smoke; a hammock, hung at eye-level, cradled a small infant (hammocks are a luxury reserved especially for infants; they also serve the practical purpose of protecting the infants from the ever-present rodents); and mats were piled in one corner—of course, there were no chairs. Eventually, I saw a small bundle in another corner of the room. It moved slightly. I looked again. "*Infermo* [sick]," the brujo said.

I walked over to the bundle, knelt down, and opened the blanket slightly. There lay a small boy about two years old. I took out my flashlight and saw that his eyes were glazed and that he was nearly comatose. "He is very, very sick," I said resignedly.

The eyes of the old man seemed to know. "Yes, I know. We will take him to the hospital tomorrow . . . *mañana*."

I covered the sick little boy again and sang softly a lullaby I often sang to my children at home. The dignified man took my hand and gently patted it. He and I were accepting. I was learning to accept the inevitable. And I was also learning that in a land where nothing is wasted, time and human effort for a lost cause also are not wasted.

The brujo showed us the rest of the compound and asked us to take a picture of him and his grandson. I took the picture, and Magdelena took one of me and the brujo. I never saw him again, as the next week was my last in Xajáxac. I did, however, send Magdelena a copy of the photograph of the brujo and me. I suspect it is somewhere in his house, perhaps casting special spells or perhaps the brujo displays it when telling stories about me—just as I am telling about him in my story. I wish I knew. There are many

El brujo and grandson in front of their house (notice the sacred maize hanging above the corredor)

others I came to know and grew to respect, but the brujo is clearly one that I respect the most.

The remaining days flew by, and soon it was time for me to leave Guatemala. The last night I was at Xajáxac, we heard a knock at the door. Our neighbors had asked us to come to their house. We entered their hut, and as my eyes adjusted to the darkness and smoke, I saw about twenty people sitting around the fire.

"They have come," Magdelena said, "to say goodbye and to thank you for coming." As would often happen, I was moved and surprised by the deep courtesy and generosity of these people. They have so little, but no kindness goes unacknowledged. In a profound sense, these people are true representatives of one of the oldest of civilizations.

The women served us a special dish of sausage wrapped in

tortillas and the hot, chocolate rice drink, atole. For a while we sat quietly on the earthen floor. Then Magdelena and I left. We slept, in peace, during my last night at Xajáxac—the place of black water and witch doctors.

Summing up the Missionary Experience: Leaving Chimaltenango

The six weeks had gone by quickly, and although I knew I had barely lessened my ignorance of a different culture, I also knew that I had changed about 180 degrees. Near the end of my stay, Doc sought me out to show me something about the Indian culture. If he saw a particularly good weaving, he would become as excited as one does upon seeing a Rembrandt and would hurry to find someone to share the beauty of it with him. That day he chose me. He, who had sent me the you're-not-welcome letter, also asked me to return to Chimaltenango—to find answers, to study the people more. During the years to follow, Doc was always my friend, always ready for conversation and challenge; he was the most charismatic man I have ever met, because he believed so deeply in the cause he was promoting.

During this six-week period in Chimaltenango I had learned to look beneath the surface, to study the issues from many sides, not to just believe one informant, but to check things out, again and again. For instance, when I first arrived, I had been told that the Behrhorst Hospital was for Indians and that Ladinos were not welcomed. After three weeks of being in the hospital, I noticed that there were always some patients dressed in Ladino clothes. When I asked about this, I was told that Ladinos could pay more and so were welcomed as paying customers. But they weren't liked. Things were said by the in-group (the Indians) that one often hears said about an out-group (in this case, the Ladinos): they're not to be trusted; they're dirty; they're diseased. Knowing that the population of Guatemala was about one-half Indian and one-half Ladino, I could not ignore the problem, for that would mean ignoring half of the population. Also, the wealth of the country was in the hands of the Ladinos, so the type of reverse discrimination I sometimes saw at the Behrhorst Hospital was in opposition to what was occurring on the larger, national scene. In order to understand the whole system, I would also need to study the Ladino culture. And this is what I did.

Zaragoza
1974 Fieldwork Begins

> I've discovered in myself a great fondness for this place—it came
> over me with a rush. We drove in with the rain pouring down
> in great white separate drops and sunlit clouds, and soft veils
> of rain sifting and forming against the far off mesas.
> —Ruth Benedict, letter on entering her fieldwork with the
>   Zuni, August 6, 1925

Leaving my suitcases in Antiqua, I drove my four-cylinder red Opel
Kadette, El Torrito (the little red bull; the name given to my car by
Guatemalan friends), up the steep volcanic mountains, past
Parramus, past Chimaltenango, the town at the crossroads, on
toward the Valley of Tecpán, site of one of the last, bloodiest battles
between Pedro de Alvarado's Conquistador Spanish Army and the
indigenous Cakchiquels in the 1580s. It was the dry season, and
the roads were rutted—dusty but passable. I had come to investigate
the possibilities of living in Zaragoza, a Ladino town in the
highlands. It was now 1974; three years had passed since I left the
Department of Chimaltenango, Xajáxac, the Behrhorst Hospital,
and the pension La Bohemia.

I had spent time preparing for the first goal of anthropologists:
the fieldwork experience that leads to a dissertation. My Spanish
had improved, because I had spent three months living with a
Spanish-speaking family in Antigua, Guatemala—part of my total
immersion experience at the Proyecto Lingüístico Marroquín, the
language and linguistic research school I mentioned earlier. In my

coursework I studied extensively the history and cultures of Central America. I focused specifically on demography, economics, the role of women, and family planning. I felt prepared to begin the field-work. I was eager to understand more deeply the lifeways of the the Guatemalan highland families and how they adapted to unending poverty, and how culture, through its system of symbols, helped shape individuals' responses to these stresses. I saw my role as an anthropologist as one of trying to piece together the mysteries of these people. I would try to learn why these people, as well as others caught in poverty in developing countries, continued to perpetuate a cycle of childbearing when so many children were destined to die in their early years of life. I carried with me the memory of my second day of work in the Behrhorst Hospital, when Baby Rosa died from malnutrition in her mother's arms. Perhaps through rigorous fieldwork I would understand this pattern of culture, this riddle of life.

A Dilemma or a Blessing?: A Family in the Field

Before delving into this riddle and the particulars of fieldwork, I needed to consider my family—my husband and two children, now eight and ten years of age. Being away from them for the six-week period I worked as a missionary nurse was more or less a snap, but now I would face being away from them for possibly a year or more. What role would my family play during this critical part of my doctoral work? I recalled that Margaret Mead, my first role model in anthropology, had a daughter, Mary Catherine Bateson, but she was born *after* Mead's active fieldwork. Where could I get advice about how to deal with this dilemma?

In searching for answers I found no role models. All of the women anthropologists cited in Peggy Golde's fascinating book, *Women in the Field* (1970), had done their fieldwork without any children. Their honest views about the vulnerability of women in the field also gave me cause to wonder if my decision was a very wise, or a very foolish, idea. The wisdom in Golde's book came from giants in the field: Laura Nader, Ernestine Friedl, Hazel Weidman, Laura Thompson, Gloria Marshall, Helen Codere, Cora duBois, Ann Fischer, Ruth Landes, Jean Biggs, and Margaret Mead herself. Nevertheless, I needed a model—a mother with children in the field—and there simply were none. Several male colleagues with families were doing their fieldwork at the time, but none had their families with them. Some female colleagues with families were doing fieldwork close to home. No one, however, was taking a family to a far-away, remote village. How could I do this? Should I even try?

Again, *we*, my family and I, answered the question—in the affirmative. My husband and our children, said yes, this should be a shared experience. We believed that it would make us wiser, stronger, and more committed citizens of the world—and it did.

The arrangements of this unusual endeavor became my responsibility. I used my wits and my social network to accomplish the job. After working as a missionary nurse with Doc Behrhorst, I remained friends with many families involved in the mission work. These families had a strong support network, and church denominations made no difference to them. One thing they talked about was home-leave. Every three or four years the church represented by a missionary family would arrange for that family to have an extended period of time back in the States.

Usually a family would return to the States for several months. During this time they needed someone to housesit their mission-field home. I was lucky to find a family that needed a housesitter for their home in Guatemala City during the summer of 1974. This mission home was spacious and comfortable—an easy transition for an American family. So, my husband, Don; our son, Paul; and Janis, our daughter, joined me that summer of 1974.

As fall approached, we needed to decide whether the children were going to return with their father (who was completing his doctoral dissertation and needed peace and quiet), or attend classes along with the village children, or attend a reputable Guatemalan boarding school with American teachers and an American curriculum. By this time I was deeply involved in my fieldwork, and I stayed in the village most of the time. I lived there exclusively from August 1974 onward. We looked carefully into the village schools: one teacher for 100 children, no chalk or chalkboards, no books. The Ladino town I was studying was Zaragoza. The Zaragoza program is one of constant memorization and recitation. The Catholic school in Patzún, my Indian town, is bilingual (Cakchiquel and Spanish)—probably too much of a transition. The boarding school in Huehuetenango was quite the opposite, with small classrooms, outstanding teachers, and excellent equipment and learning resources. After lots of discussion, visits, and thought, we decided to enroll the children in the Huehuetenango Academy for the fall semester and take them back to Colorado in December. I would return to Guatemala, alone, in 1975. The children were ecstatic with the decision. In their eyes, Huehuetenango was open fields to run in, streams to cross, and the majestic Chuchumachanes Mountains to climb.

It was the right decision, but not an easy one. I spent eight hours of rough driving, every two weeks, into the rugged mountains near the Mexico border to visit the children. We all grew homesick at times, but my fieldwork got done, the children met lifelong friends in both villages and also in the boarding school, and Don completed his doctoral studies. Coming face-to-face with educational impoverishment in developing countries is a grief experience, as one mourns that millions of minds are stunted in their growth and potential for lack of books, chalk, and hope—but we felt, right or wrong, that we couldn't submit our children's future to that sad reality.

Discovering Zaragoza

In order to find answers to the questions and mysteries I mentioned earlier in the chapter, I planned to do a controlled comparative study, looking at two different societies—a Ladino town and an Indian town—that are similar in many ways, but also culturally different, in order to learn whether there are any differences in the number of children each family has, and if so, why. Individual behavior, such as sexual reproduction, varies within societies; however, there are norms, rules, and values that societies promote through each of the social institutions (family, health, religion, education, economics, and power and politics) which mold and shape individual responses. Anthropologists refer to these lifeways as a distinctive, complex pattern known as *ethos.* Would the ethos of one culture be so different from another that the rate of reproduction might be affected? Or would the differences be such that other patterns of family formation might appear distinctive? I planned to find answers to these questions.

My experiences living in the highlands with the Cakchiquel gave me a base line from which to find another type of culture for comparison. It was by persistently reading ethnographies about Guatemala that I discovered Zaragoza, a "peculiar" Ladino town, in the predominantly Indian highlands. Remember, in 1971 the Department of Chimaltenango had a population that was 77.6 percent Indian; thus, any Ladinos living in the department were a noticeable minority. So why would there be a town of Ladinos in a predominantly Indian region? Alfredo Mendéz, a Guatemalan anthropologist, had studied the Ladino town during the 1960s and wrote a book on his work in 1967. I read the book thoroughly and knew from the description that this town would certainly be different from the predominantly Indian towns I had encountered. I met Mendéz in his office at the University of San Carlos in

Guatemala City and discussed my plan for a comparative study; he strongly supported my proposal.

The Breadth and Depth of Ladino Power

In the Behrhorst Hospital, I had gotten to know a few Ladinos, but I wanted to know, not conjecture about, what their world is really like. I began to read the works of Richard Adams (1970), who has written extensively about the Ladinos. I have already mentioned the Ladinos' Spanish and Mayan background. The major distinction between the Indian and Ladino in Guatemala is socioeconomic. The Indian usually lives in the rural highlands, engages in agriculture, speaks a Mayan language, dresses in indigenous, hand-woven clothing, and usually practices folk catholicism. The Ladino, on the other hand, lives primarily in the big urban centers, such as Guatemala City, which in 1974 had more than a million inhabitants. The Ladino speaks Spanish, wears Westernized clothing, is educated, and engages in commerce. Ladinos are predominantly Roman Catholic and practice *compadrazgo*, a formal system of godparenting.

The Ladino system influences all of the social organizations of Guatemala. Religion, education, the economy, and the military—all are controlled by Ladinos. In contrast, the Indian system is locally based; there are no Indian organizations at the national level. When I began my fieldwork in 1974, there were no written Mayan languages nor had they been transliterated into Spanish or English. At one time, the Maya had a written language, but only five pieces of evidence remain; the rest were destroyed during the Spanish Conquest (mainly by Catholic priests who labeled them as pagan writings). The Popul Vuh, the sacred book of the Quiché Maya of Guatemala, is the most famous of the five. It was transcribed not in the Quiché language, but in Latin, around A.D. 1560 by an unknown, but highly literate Quiché Mayan Indian (Goetz and Morley, 1950). *The Annuals of the Cakchiquel* is an ancient book about the Cakchiquel that was translated into Latin. A third book, translated by the famous scholar of the Maya, Bishop Landa, is the *Book of the Chilam Balam*. The title is derived from the native prophet who had written about the treacheries of the Maya and who also predicted the arrival of the Spaniards from the east (Coe, 1969:117).

Since the 1970s, several Mayan-language dictionaries have been produced; much of the work has been done by Wycliffe Bible translators and other scholar-linguists, such as those from the

Proyecto Lingüístico Marroquín in Antigua. During my experiences in Guatemala, I met few Indians who were interested in learning to read and write in a Mayan language; however, the majority, including women, wanted to become literate in Spanish, for Spanish is the language for trade above the local level.

The Settling of New Spain

Understanding how Latin America had been populated is an important piece of history that would place into context what I was to discover in my fieldwork. The first settlers, the Indians, traveled across the Bering Strait from areas of what is now Asia in about 25,000 B.C. (Mörner, 1970:9). The geographical variation created *population isolates*, groups of people separated by natural barriers. This isolation gave rise to cultural diversity among the groups. In Central and South America more than 123 linguistic families have been documented, and in Mexico and Guatemala alone there are 260 languages (Mörner, 1970). In spite of the diversity, great societies arose: first the Maya, then the Aztec, and finally the Inca. Each represented a society more complex than the one that preceded it. The pre-Columbian population of Latin America was estimated by the historian, Angel Rosenblat (1967), to have been 13 million. Another historian, Woodrow Wilson Borah (1963), estimated it at 100 million. This wide discrepancy in the estimates is likely because most records were destroyed by the Spanish priests, who believed that the indigenous inhabitants were a pagan people. Whatever the estimate, it is apparent that there were more native inhabitants in Latin America than there were to the north, in what is now the United States. Consequently, the conquering of Latin America was far different from the pioneering efforts of families in North America. The advanced civilizations and concentrated populations of Mexico and Central America meant force was met with counterforce as the Spanish conquistadores marched from the east coast of Mexico through the southern areas and into today's Guatemala.

It is also important to remember that the culture brought to the New World by the Spanish was already heterogenous. For 700 years there had been a combination of coexistence, inbreeding, and acculturation between the Christians, Muslims, and Jews on the Iberian Peninsula (Mörner, 1970). Magnus Mörner believes that the prevailing cultural traits of the conquistadores stemmed from Moorish influence. For instance, the five centuries of struggle between the Christians and Muslims had left a population with a rebellious, warlike way of life. This struggle also created a class of military men who regarded manual labor and commerce with disgust. The Moorish Wars, with their crusading character, engendered a religious fanaticism and a chivalrous, compensating spirit, illustrated, for example, by El Cid, the celebrated Spanish hero of the Middle Ages. This same spirit was again displayed in the New World, giving sanction to the conquest of what the conquistadores believed were the New World pagans.

The indigenous women were the first to be overcome in the path of the conquistadores in the New World. The conquistadores' pattern of seizure was very different from the pattern of the migrating and settling, pioneer families to the north, who tended to isolate themselves from the natives. During the conquest, native women were given as gifts to appease the conquistadores or were taken by force; seldom were indigenous women "wooed and won." This so-called exchange of women was vital in easing the tensions between the Spaniards and the indigenous people. The Catholic church, disapproving, but still realistic about the conquering forces, demanded that the native women be "baptized before coition." Consequently, some of the conquistadores viewed their acts of aggression as some type of Christian mission (Mörner, 1970:25).

The first Mayan-Spanish descendants were called *mestizos*, a term still used in Mexico. Guatemalan mestizos were considered the legal heirs of the conquistadores; their descendants became the Ladino group in Guatemala. As lenient as the Catholic church was in these cases, the Spanish crown was reluctant to make the offspring legal heirs, as that only meant the property would be divided, and the crown would have less. The king and queen of Spain feared loss of control over their new possessions; thus, they ushered in a complicated system to measure inheritance: scales of social status. Early in the 1700s a nomenclature of castes, reflecting descent, was developed. It contained as many as sixteen restrictive categories. As an example, if a woman in the class of *chamiss* (the exact meaning of the word has been lost) and a mestizo man (indigenous and Spanish) married, their offspring would be given the class title *coyote mestizo*. Then, to take the classification system even further, if a coyote mestizo man and a mulatto woman married, their child would be termed *ahi te estas*. This cumbersome, stigmatizing system became too complex to be manageable and was eventually incorporated into a corresponding social status system (Mörner, 1970:60). This social status system still exists in some sectors of Guatemalan society, where heritage is key to transcending the social ladder. In these sectors, one is likely to hear the recitation of a person's lineage in various social settings or see lineages in print in society sections of some newspapers.

Suppression of the Indigenous People as Land Is Divided

Soon after the arrival of the conquistadores the Spanish crown began dividing the indigenous peoples' land among the settlers, (that is, the conquistadores). Those people who had already lived in Latin America, perhaps for centuries, were forced from their land or made subject to the new landowners. This system was called *encomiendo* and remained until late in the eighteenth century, when a newly reformed, yet still oppressive, system, a peonage, was begun. Indigenous people, now relegated to a low caste position, were required by law to work a certain number of days in the mines and vast fincas for a very small wage. The rich owner, or the *patron*, further indentured the natives through a system of loans that could not be repaid. This system was supported by the church and remains even today, in spite of the fact that revolutions have occurred over the past hundred years—and even within the past twenty years—resulting in numerous efforts to establish equitable rights and to reform land-ownership conditions. Today many of the large finca owners do not even live in Latin America but are residents of other countries, including the United States; yet they extract their wealth from the backs of the natives. Basically, the social structure of Latin America remains a dual class system, and in Guatemala it remains a division between the Ladinos and the Indians, with the Indians occupying the inferior position.

The land situation in Guatemala was made even more inequitable in the late nineteenth century when the government expropriated 2.5 million acres of land and turned them over to German immigrants for profitable coffee production. As a part of the expropriation, thousands of peasants were forcibly removed and sometimes killed (Simon, 1987:20). A light began to glimmer toward rectifying this inequality when two democratic presidents were elected: Dr. Juan José Arévalo (1945–51) and Jacobo Arbenz Guzmán (1951–54). Their years in office are sometimes called the "ten years of spring." President Arévalo abolished the Vagrancy Law, which forced any peasant with less than ten acres of land to perform unpaid service to land owners (this service was accountable and recorded in passbooks). Arévalo also introduced a social security system and legalized labor unions and cooperatives. Other reforms he instituted included literacy programs and building of rural schools.

President Arbenz also was a reformer. He is most noted for initiating a land reform that expropriated idle lands and unionized even more of the population. One of the strongest opponents to the land reform was the United Fruit Company of the United States, which had a monopoly on the banana industry since 1901. In June 1954, so-called Liberation Forces led an attack against Arbenz, who was forced to resign on June 27, 1954. Colonel Carlos Castillo Armas became the next president (Simon, 1987:25). Since that time, the country has remained largely unstable. This history of Guatemala is widely recorded, so in this ethnography I will not dwell on the political strife but rather on how the people in each of the towns I have studied have coped with their day-to-day living within a context of a poor, developing, unstable national economy.

The perpendicular nature of Guatemala, with its high volcanic peaks and low coastal lands, make it a land where people are isolated geographically. This isolation creates great cultural diversity. For this reason, I decided to study not one town, but two quite different towns that are located only ten kilometers apart: Zaragoza and Patzún.

Establishing the First Research Site

How did a group of Ladinos, a minority living among the Cakchiquel Indians, come to this region? The exact story is unlikely to be known, but several versions have been proposed. One version is that soldiers of Pedro de Alvarado's army became disenchanted and deserted their conquistador leader. They eventually settled in the fertile valley of Zaragoza to begin new lives in New Spain (Mendéz, 1967). The other version states that a group of gypsies, originally from the area of Zaragoza, Spain, came as early settlers to Guatemala and confiscated the land from the indigenous people (Adams, 1964). According to the public records, forty-seven Spaniards founded the town in A.D. 1731. A legend says they named it for a Spanish princess, Zara, who was a member of their group. Zara liked the flat valley (*goza* means "she enjoys") and wanted to make it her home. It is far more likely, however, that the town was named for Zaragoza, the province in Spain. Zaragoza is 7,200 feet above sea level and sixty-two kilometers from the capital. In 1974 it had a population of about 3,300 people. As I mentioned above, the true story of the settlement may never be known, and it probably doesn't matter; what is apparent, as I was to discover, is that the residents of Zaragoza are very different from Indians living in the surrounding areas.

Driving up the mountains and toward the town, my mind wandered back over the years, and I recalled passing by Zaragoza on the highway to Xajáxac. I remembered glancing out the window of the Blue Bird, a few kilometers outside Chimaltenango, and seeing a lush, beautiful valley with brightly colored houses—pinks, blues, greens, and yellows—neatly lined in straight rows, and the gleaming-white tombstones in a cemetery near the highway. I had asked Magdelena, "What is the name of that town?"

"It's Zaragoza *muy feo*, [very ugly]," she had replied, making a face. "Ladinos, *muy sucio*." I had wondered if she meant that literally—"very unclean"—or was referring to the out-group, "those who are different than we are," a common way of distinguishing between "us" and "them." I was to find out that both meanings applied.

As I neared the cemetery, I saw a dirt road leading to the center of town. I drove onto the rutted lane and down toward the plaza as my Opel jerked and bolted over the deep ruts left by the last year's rains. My goal was to find a place to live for a year, a field site. I hoped for a vacant house that I could furnish.

The town was well laid out in the customary Spanish design. The houses were all connected as if they were one long wall of different colors, and each small unit was topped with a red-tiled roof. There were only two main streets, which divided the town into four quarters. The cemetery was located on the highest point in the town; the next highest point housed the tall steeple of the Catholic church, which dominated the central plaza. There was a park in the center of the plaza, but it contained neither running water, nor flowers, nor grass. Its two main features were the pathways that crisscrossed the area and the basketball hoops located at the two ends of one side. Opposite the cathedral stood a one-story building labeled with the sign Municipio; I assumed it was the official headquarters of the town, where I would find the *alcalde* (mayor) and the clerks. Next to the municipal building were the post office and telegraph office. The next building was low and long, and also deserted. I learned that this building weekly housed a market, but a poor one with only a handful of vendors and a meager selection of produce. A small tienda was situated on a corner of the plaza, and there I saw the only bit of life in the whole town—an older woman standing behind a counter.

I pulled my car up to the tienda, and with some trembling from anticipation, walked toward the older woman. As I drew closer I saw piercing black eyes, almost defiant and defensive. She did not smile, nor did she speak. Her black shawl was drawn tightly over her head and across her back. She looked wrinkled, but powerful. My eyes glanced at the wares in the small store: pins, thread, candy, flour, yard goods, aspirin, Alka-Seltzer, soda pop, cigarettes, small toys, and a piñata—in general, things needed for modern lives. A small transistor radio played Spanish songs, very loudly.

"I would like some orange juice," my voice squeaked, "and some *dulces* [sweets], please." The black-shawled woman reached swiftly toward the items and handed them to me, saying only, "*Cuarenta centavos*" (Forty cents).

I thought the price was right and gave her the correct change. I opened the can of juice and slowly drank it; then I opened the candy wrapper and slowly chewed the candy, looking around the area. How am I going to ask about living here? I wondered. As I searched for the right words, my thoughts were interrupted by the appearance of a young, handsome man emerging from the schoolhouse.

He came directly to me, smiling, and said, "Good morning, I am Jorge Martínez, the principal of the school. Are you visiting the area?"

I knew he must have been very suspicious of me, as Americans and European tourists would not get off the main highway and enter Zaragoza unless they were lost. I knew it was an opportunity to make or break my fieldwork, as I could see this was the exact place where I wanted to live.

"Yes, I am Juanita; I have just come from Antigua, where I have been studying Spanish. I am a student from the United States, and I am looking for a place to live in this area."

Jorge looked a bit surprised, but not shocked. He did not ask about my studies. "What kind of place do you want to live in and for how long will you stay?"

"I have two children and a husband, so I need a place that's big enough for all of us. My husband is a teacher, too, and he will be returning to the States in a few months to work, and my children will go to school in Huehuetenango. I will be here for about a year or so. I thought that if anyone had a small house to rent, that would be just right for us."

He smiled, as if he understood what I needed. He began speaking quickly and quietly to the woman in the black shawl. They looked at me now and then. He said, "Let me talk it over with some of the teachers." Jorge then disappeared into the school again. In a few minutes three attractive women, who were obviously teachers, emerged. They were talking rapidly to each other, and all greeted me warmly. I realized I was quite a mystery. In the meantime, the woman in the black shawl peered over the counter at me, and she did not smile. I knew I was being judged, so I stood tall and erect.

Next the women and Jorge huddled with the woman in the black shawl. I was obviously the topic of conversation. The women went back into the school, waving good-bye, and the old woman came around the side of the tienda, closed the window, and locked the door. She was less than five feet tall, with a beautiful face, wrinkled with time, and a crown of black wavy hair with a silver streak framing one side of her forehead. As she talked, I saw deep dimples in her cheeks. It seemed I'd seen her before, in pictures of gypsies in southern Europe.

"I am Silvia Marquez; my husband's name is Pablo, and I [she didn't say "we"] have a house to rent," she said matter-of-factly.

Jorge seemed pleased. "You are very lucky," he said.

"May I see your house, please?" I asked excitedly.

"Yes, follow me," said the beautiful, gypsy woman. "Follow me."

Out of her pocket she pulled a large ring of keys and proceeded to lead me across the street to a pink house with blue trim. It had two doors, each of which led into separate, large rectangular rooms. The walls in each of these rooms were filled with calendars with pictures of saints on them. The floor was gray cement. The roof looked like corrugated steel; I imagined it would keep us safe, but become hot in the summer and noisy in the rainy season. We walked through one room, and then Silvia opened another door that led to a spacious patio and a corridor with plants along the wall. The *pila* (water trough) dominated the backyard; it was very big, almost like a small swimming pool, I thought. Next to the pila was a room, where I spied a *sink*—with running water. I could hardly believe it. I had expected to go to the central fountain or stream for my water supply, but here I would have running water—a virtual miracle! Next to the kitchen was another room, the latrine, with an open pit, and another room with a shower. More than I could have ever hoped for! All my requirements were met—water, a latrine, and even electricity. The doors seemed fragile, but safe, and the one window in the living room was secure, with bars on it.

I pondered what it would be like here as the only gringa. (I was later to learn another American woman lived in Zaragoza on the outskirts of town, but she was considered a witch.) Would I be able to learn the lifeways? Yes! Within eyesight and earshot were the cathedral, the municipal buildings, the school, the market, and the plaza. I was ecstatic, as to observe and participate, a fieldworker must be accessible to all the events of a culture.

"How much is the rent?" I asked.

"Fifteen quetzales [the equivalent of fifteen U.S. dollars] a month," she replied, "plus $1.50 for electricity."

"I will pay you for four months today, and I would like to move

Silvia Marquez, fictive mother of author, a resourceful businessperson

in over the weekend, if that is all right with you," I said hopefully.

The gypsy woman nodded and walked quickly toward another building, which I would learn was her main store and also her residence with her husband, Pablo, and her two daughters, Antonia, twenty-two years old, and Victoria, twenty-five. Silvia produced a receipt book and wrote out the transaction; she was a businesswoman. As the years went by, Silvia, her husband, and their daughters became my best friends and fictive family. It was through them, mainly, that I learned of the lifeways of the Ladinos of Zaragoza. Several months after my arrival in Zaragoza Silvia revealed to me that when I first appeared in her tienda, she had felt that I was a special messenger from God but was glad to learn that I was just an ordinary person. This may have seemed naive to me at one time. But as I lived with her in the context of her culture, I found her wise beyond belief, brave, and very intelligent.

That weekend I moved into my new home, *la casa de la gringa*, as it became known. I painted the inside walls white and the gray cement floor a bright red. I placed grass mats like area rugs around the room, to soften the harshness. A Catholic priest and friend sold me his propane cooking stove for twenty dollars. I found I needed a false ceiling in the kitchen to protect my lungs from the heavy smoke of my neighbor's open-fire cooking. I stapled long pieces of green plastic sheeting on the rafters high over my head and that kept me smoke-free. I bought local furniture: a sitting bench, chairs, a table, and two cots with small, hard mattresses. On the walls I put pictures of Guatemalan people and scenery. On the patio I hung a large hammock and placed many plants around the area. It looked like home to me. My husband would later bring a pressure cooker for making the local water safe to drink. I shopped locally at various vendors, buying carrots, potatoes, rice, tomatoes, and occasionally beef and my daily supply of tortillas. There was no market day, such as I had known in Chimaltenango, and since I had no refrigerator, I had to buy everything daily. I grew slender during that year on such a wholesome diet, and I also remained clean and frisky, taking daily cold showers, outdoors near the pila. About once a month I would go to Guatemala City and indulge in a pizza and beer and maybe a McDonald's hamburger. Once a week I would drive to Chimaltenango and have supper with my friends from the Behrhorst Clinic; however, my life that year was spent primarily in two towns: Zaragoza and my Indian town of choice, Patzún.

Chapter 7

Patzún
A Town of Indian Power

> Our people will never be scattered. Our destiny will triumph over
> the ill-fated days which are coming at a time unknown. We will
> always be secure in the land we have occupied.
> —the Popul Vuh

Patzún, known as a town of Indian power, or Red Power, is a world
apart from the town just left, Zaragoza, yet it is only ten kilometers
away on an asphalt highway. The stability of cultural patterns in
Patzún is a mystery. One can't help wondering why the *patzuñeros*
continue doing the same things century after century.
Understanding such patterns, or riddles, comes only with careful,
patient study. Was Patzún, this Indian town, known to insiders and
outsiders alike as a town where the indigenous people are in power,
to be my second research site? I made this important decision only
after I had explored and evaluated several similar towns: San
Marcos in the north, Comalápa to the west, and Sololá to the east.
I studied the geographical layout and such obvious sociocultural
structures as churches, schools, and markets in each of these towns.
Zaragoza was the only Ladino town in the department, but there
were several predominantly Indian towns in the highlands that
could be used as a comparison. I wanted to choose the one that was
most similar to Zaragoza in size and in other ways. After spending
a couple weeks in study, I knew that Patzún was the most similar
to Zaragoza. Additionally, Patzún was much closer to Zaragoza than

79

the other comparable Indian towns. Since I planned to take daily trips for comparison, Patzún was a wise choice.

Different Values, Different Norms

Patzún means "the sign of the bull," and the town is named for the leather products coming from this area (ironically, I never saw any cattle and glimpsed only a few pigs). Probably founded around the twelfth century, the township of Patzún was part of the empire of the Cakchiquel Mayan Indians and, because of its location in the center of rich, volcanic mountains, was a leading trade center in the highlands before the Spaniards arrived in A.D.1530 (Morales, 1961). Almost since its beginning, Patzún has been known as a center of Indian power. Perhaps this is because it forms a natural crossroads between various mountains and trade routes to the coast; perhaps it is due to the richness of the land in the area, which could have fostered its development and wealth. Or perhaps its power is related to certain key leaders who emerged from that area. Whatever the reasons, it is a powerful town and was known in 1974 as Red Power. It was common to hear people exclaim that the next president of Guatemala would be patzuñero. I think that Patzún's power base is likely due to a combination of all three factors: trade routes, rich land, and leadership.

The population of Patzún is 6,400—slightly greater than the population of Zaragoza (3,300)—and, like Zaragoza, Patzún is an agricultural town (75 percent of its inhabitants are subsistence farmers). The major crop grown in Patzún is corn, the sacred maize. The patzuñero is a far better farmer than the *zaragozaño*. There is no simple answer to why this is so, but the difference is documented in many studies. The farmers themselves do not comment on this difference, and the only possible answer I can surmise after living there for a year is that the Indian has a different cultural value toward land and farming. Chapter 1 of this book mentions that the Moors did not favor physical labor, so perhaps the Spanish conquistadores brought with them a distaste for farming; they valued other things more highly. Also patzuñeros are risk takers, eager to try new crops and new ideas; this is not so for the zaragozaños, who are very conservative and not inclined to experiment. In 1974 Patzún had two agricultural extension agencies, and a Peace Corps volunteer taught the local people how to grow fruit trees and other new crops. Zaragoza had neither of these. Patzún had six cooperatives for men and three for women to help the patzuñeros market their crops and weavings with less overhead and more profit. Zaragoza had none.

The values, beliefs, and attitudes of the Indians of Patzún are unlike those of the Zaragoza Ladinos; I sensed the differences the moment I drove into town. In many towns, even though Indians are the majority, they are not in power, but in Patzún, they were. All the town's elected officials were Indian: the mayor, the town clerk, and all the councilmen. Yes, this was a different town.

The Town's Vibrancy and Energy

My first trip into Patzún was filled with expectation. I now was settled into my Zaragoza house, and I wanted to find a home in Patzún. But where to start? Driving the winding, narrow, and dangerous Pan-American Highway made me vigilant, as it is nicknamed the Ribbon of the Seven Deadly Sins, because so many people have lost their lives on it. At points, the curves are so sharp that the highway almost makes a 180 degree turn. It is treacherous, especially on first acquaintance! As I finally drove off the highway and into the outskirts of town, I observed the patzuñeros walking along the side of the road and in the streets. The women were dressed in bright-red huipiles with intricate blue-and-white embroidery along the necklines. I thought they were the most beautiful huipiles in all of Guatemala. The women's faldas were equally colorful, bright-blue-striped wraparounds. (Those who have seen photographs of the 1992 Nobel laureate, Rigoberta Menchú, may recall seeing her wearing the red-and-blue traje of Patzún.) The men and young boys were dressed in stark black-and-white embroidered wool jackets, white knee-length pantalones, and a white or black apronlike garment across the front. Each man's head was covered with a white straw hat, and most carried large machetes in their belts, one to each man. The patzuñeros were striking, especially with their straight black hair and high cheekbones. Most were barefoot, but some wore heavy sandals made from old automobile tires. (In some coastal resorts, this item sells for quite a sum of money—in the name of ecology. The patzuñeros were *living* ecology, not marketing it.)

Instead of the straight streets of Zaragoza, Patzún had winding, narrow streets, and the town was very hilly and windy. No one seemed to pay any attention to me; they were accustomed to seeing tourists driving from the Pan-American Highway, through their town, and toward the beautiful, volcanic Lake Atitlán, about forty kilometers to the northeast. I drove directly toward the center of town, using the magnificent cathedral, with its numerous steeples, as my guide. (It is one of the most beautiful and famous cathedrals in all of Guatemala.) Parking my car by a curbed sidewalk, I walked to the center of the town, where a large fountain was spouting water. People were milling around, although it was not a true market day. Flowers were everywhere. A few women were selling vegetables and fruits arranged on plastic sheets on the ground—a setup similar to the large market I attended in Chimaltenango. I bargained for some tomatoes and potatoes; the prices were right and the quality excellent. There were only women vendors, and they seemed self-confident and open, unlike the quiet, modest Indian women I had seen three years earlier in Chimaltenango. Again, I learned how important it is *not to stereotype people*—not even if one is a supposed virtuoso. Not *all* Indian women are modest and quiet, nor are *all* Ladinos aggressive and immodest. Rather, one must see the groups within the context of their own values, norms, and behaviors, and one must also see the *individuals* within each group.

The confidence of the townspeople made me feel very comfortable. I knew I would like living in Patzún. As it was nearly noon when I drove into town, I didn't go into the cathedral, but saved that event for another day. I wanted to find a place to rent, so I drove my car to the Colégio San Bernardino, the famous school for Cakchiquel children and youths, hoping to meet someone who could help me with my search.

A Spanish Priest and Two American Nuns

Padre Sergio, from Spain, who founded the boarding school over twenty-five years ago, is well known throughout the region for his social programs. Although he is not considered a revolutionary, his programs are meant to change the lives of the Indian people. Children, grades one through nine, *both males and females*, are taught to read and write Spanish. Most rural schools teach through sixth grade only, and many through third only. The students at Colégio San Bernardino also learn technical skills, such as mechanics, typing, and sewing. I had heard that two American nuns were helping Padre Sergio in the boarding school, and I wanted to meet them. Perhaps I would learn from them whether any Patzún family would be willing to rent me a room for an extended period of time—most likely a year.

As I drove near the Colégio I could see that classes were being dismissed for lunch; children were piling out of the buildings, some going home and others going to a cafeteria. It looked busy. I approached the large main building and went up some steps. There

I encountered a beautiful young nun in a navy blue dress. Her hair was light brown, and her smile filled her face; I knew she was an American. "Hi," I said. "My name is JoAnn. I'm from Colorado."

"Oh, I'm so glad to meet you!" she replied in an accent that was pure Wisconsin. "I'm Sonia, and I heard that you were living in Zaragoza, and we had hoped that you would stop and meet us— me, Christiana, and Padre. Won't you have lunch with us? We were just about to begin, and we always have an extra plate waiting for guests."

It was one of the most memorable luncheons I have ever been to. We talked like old friends, laughing about some of our common early-adjustment experiences in Guatemala. Padre Sergio had a great sense of humor and delighted in telling stories of his arrival by car twenty-five years earlier. "When I honked my horn to warn people of my coming, the crowds would only grow larger, and larger: they all wanted to see this car!" For several hours we talked about the common problems of the Indians and the hope for the future that they all shared.

"The only hope is through education—teaching them to read and write in Spanish; they are a proud people and very practical. They know the only way to link with the national economy is through the ability to market in the dominant language. But in their homes, they are pure naturales," Padre explained.

The American nuns, Sonia and Christiana, had been with the boarding school for nine years. "We have seen the Indian women, especially, grow more independent and resourceful. They have found strength in numbers and in working together in cooperatives. These cooperatives grew out of the *cofradia* system, which as you know is a ceremonial social system that links the religious community into various hierarchies. The old system has broken down, as the *fiesta* system was difficult to follow in a modern society. But that fiesta system grew into cooperatives, when they became legal (in the 1960s) and it is a far more productive way of organizing," explained Christiana, who seemed to have an interest in the economy of Guatemala.

When I asked whether they knew of any family in town from whom I could rent a room for my studies, they all chimed in, "Live here with us." I laughed and explained that living in such luxury and speaking English all the time wouldn't serve the purpose of getting to know the people's lifeways. They laughed, too, and simultaneously said, "Why not the Maczuls?" They explained that this family was well known in town and was a very typical large family living in a compound setting. How lucky, I thought, and what a contrast to where I was living in Zaragoza. With that, Sister Sonia offered to go with me and introduce me to the family, and perhaps interpret my goals. Was I lucky!

The Maczul Family and a Compound Family Home

We drove to the Maczul family compound about three miles away, up and down the hills. I couldn't help but notice that the color of all the houses was pure brown adobe; there was no paint. However, the roofs were red-tiled, as is typical of houses in the highlands. I also saw a few cane huts along the way. As we stopped in front of the house, I noticed that the compound house was also a tienda and thought that this was similar to Silvia's business in Zaragoza. Perhaps business-minded people welcome opportunities to increase their income by renting out rooms and houses and running tiendas.

As we entered the tienda, an older woman, her long hair woven into a braid and tied with yellow ribbons, welcomed Sister Sonia. A small granddaughter was sitting on a wooden stool near the grandmother. Sonia and the older woman exchanged some niceties, and then Sonia explained, in Cakchiquel, who I was and why I wanted to live in Patzún. "Would you have a room for her to rent, so that she could eat and sleep here when she wants to stay in Patzún?" Sonia inquired for me. "Other times she will be living in Zaragoza."

The store owner looked at me with open interest. Her manner was quite unlike the suspicion I encountered in my first meeting with Silvia in Zaragoza. "I think we have a small room, just for sleeping, that you might like to see," Mother Maczul said matter-of-factly, and with that comment, she motioned for us to enter the compound house.

The house was a simple, wide-open courtyard with a pila on one end, and a series of bedrooms around the courtyard. There were about six bedrooms, no living room, no dining room. Bench-type chairs were placed against one wall. I saw two open-fire hearths on one side of the courtyard and a third on the other side. I also noticed some open windows framed by shutters on all sides. The roof extended over the courtyard, protecting the walkways on all sides. I saw no place for food storage, although I couldn't see into some of the darker corners.

My room was simple; it reminded me of my room at La Bohemia several years earlier. It comprised a bed and a small table and some open shelves. No chair. The walls were bare, except for one picture of the Virgin Mary. I noticed a bare-bulb light in the middle of the ceiling, meaning I could write at night. "I think this will serve just

Some of the members of the Maczul family (notice the Western wear of the younger males and the smiles)

fine, thank you," I said frankly. "How much is the rent per month?"

Mother Maczul replied without question, "It will be five quetzales a month."

I was delighted with such a good price and such a friendly owner. "I will be glad to pay that amount. Can I cook with someone or is there a *comedor* [eating place in a private home] nearby?" Many families choose to eat with other families, in comedores, as a way of pooling resources. For instance, one family may not own a table and another may not own a stove; a comedore allows them to come together and share a table and a stove without incurring the costs of purchasing new ones. It is common to have five or six people coming and going for meals at various times, as most families have maids whose job it is to do just the cooking.

(I hasten to clarify a perception, which may be held in the United States, that maids are associated with the very high standard of living of the rich and famous. This luxury is not the case in many developing countries where maids—or, to use a common term in Guatemala, *muchachas*—are part of a labor-intensive system of exchange. This simply means that a lot of people—and in reference to maids, young women—are employed for very low wages and meager, if any, benefits for doing quite menial jobs, such as peeling potatoes or fetching water. This employment, even at very low wages, may be the difference in some families between making it or starving and living in the street. Having had maids while living in Guatemala City, I can attest that the system is not one I admire, as the wages are so low and the workers have little opportunity to advance their education or other employment. However, in the absence of modern household appliances and transportation, as in the developing countries, someone, a human being, must do the chores necessary for daily living.)

Mother Maczul replied, "You may cook with me and my husband, if you would like. Or there is a neighbor who has a comedor; so you may want to ask her." Again, I felt fortunate, but I also knew that my experiences living in a pension and also my experiences living with several families during the total immersion program in Antigua had prepared me for a less-ordered, but highly productive, adaptive lifestyle. I knew that I could just come and go as I pleased, since flexibility is inherent in a system without means of keeping things on schedule. Far from being laissez faire, the Indians and Ladinos are hard-working, frugal people. Having rigid schedules is in many ways counterproductive in a society that needs to be able to handle a vast number of unexpected events, such as a breakdown in the electrical service or a washout of a bridge. And since most of highland Guatemala is without telephone service, it is even more difficult to deal with unforeseen circumstances. Flexibility is imperative in an unpredictable system.

I paid Mother Maczul for six months' rent, and then Sonia and I said good-bye. "How can I thank you for helping me find this wonderful family?" I had earnestly asked Sister Sonia.

"I'm just glad I could help," she replied. While driving back to the Colégio, Sonia suddenly became uneasy. "If you want to get back to Zaragoza tonight, you'd better leave right away, as it is nearly five o'clock," she said in a worried tone. "The fog sets in about five, and you won't be able to see the side of the road as you return."

I later learned the wisdom of her advice. Twice during the fieldwork I got stuck driving on the Ribbon of the Seven Deadly Sins after the evening fog had set in, and I could hardly maneuver the car for fear of going down one of the deep ravines. I had thankfully avoided the fog on my first trip back from Patzún. That evening my mind raced with thoughts and images from earlier in the day. As I entered the straight but rutted streets of Zaragoza and drove to my pink and blue house, I had the staggering feeling that I had a lot to learn about two very different cultures.

Chapter 8

The Fiesta of Corpus Christi
Symbols and Norms in Zaragoza

> Cultural knowledge represents a tradition of semantic
> ethnography embedded in a cognitive view of culture focusing
> on a system of symbols used in the social world of human beings.
> —Agnes Aamodt, Toward Conceptualizations in Nursing,
>   1992

Looking up at the ceiling of my cozy Zaragoza house, I felt I must just lie in bed a few more minutes before jumping up and running out to take a cold shower on the patio. A familiar recording of "Jesus Christ, Super Star" was blasting from a loud speaker in the cathedral, the music customarily heard on Sunday mornings. I was at ease, quite unlike my first Sunday in Zaragoza when the blast startled me from a deep sleep.

When I first went to mass in Zaragoza, the Catholic priest from Italy had told me, "I play that song, as loudly as possible, so the message will reach the whole valley, and especially those heathen *evangélicos* [evangelicals]. They're our enemies, you know; we must cast them out!" And the blasting music supposedly was one way to do so. Mendéz describes this friction between the Catholic and evangelical churches as being only "political" (Mendéz, 1967:178). The evangelical members are a very small minority in Zaragoza; they are a larger group in Patzún. During my fieldwork experience, I found Padre Sergio of Patzún to be a far more open, compassionate priest than Padre Pius of Zaragoza. Padre Pius was a man of about fifty years of age, born in Italy, and placed in

Zaragoza in the 1960s. It was obvious from talking with the people of Zaragoza that the padre did not like living there; in fact, he lived in Patzicía, about five kilometers from Zaragoza. Padre Pius was never seen in the streets of the town or outside the walls of the cathedral. I paid him a courtesy call when I first arrived and sensed that he cared very little about the social and physical well-being of the people. "The laws of the church tell us that women are to have as many children as God wishes for them. They are to be obedient to their husbands and to remain *mujeres muy decente* [very pure, decent women]." In contrast, Padre Sergio of Patzún talked about the need for women to become literate and conscious of their own well-being and supported such practices as limiting, or at least spacing, the number of children they had—he favored the rhythm method of birth control (noting signs of being in the fertile phase of ovulation and abstaining from sex during that period). Padre Sergio was often found talking with the patzuñeros—in the plaza, in the schoolyard, and everywhere else. The contrast between the two religious leaders was significant.

Ideal Male and Female Sex Roles

I was now fully awakened from the second playing of the energetic song. Finally I bounced to my feet, knowing that today was to be a special day in Zaragoza—it was the fiesta of Corpus Christi. Although this was not Sunday, the celebration would begin with a mass, followed by a procession to the chapels of each *cantón* (geographical division). In the evening the townspeople would crown the Queen of Zaragoza, then there would be some political speeches, and finally the dance. I looked forward to it all. It was June; I had been in the field for almost three months; certainly this would be an opportunity to see everyone in the town and to learn so much.

I hurried with my shower, icy cold as ever, and scurried into my kitchen to catch my breath. The mornings were very cold at these altitudes (7,200 feet above sea level in Zaragoza and 8,000 in Patzún). I knew I would not forget the shock of this daily ritual and how difficult it was to get the shampoo out of my long hair with cold water. Remember, I would say to myself, a hot shower is a luxury in life. Don't forget that. Three-fourths or more of this world's population never gets to experience such a pleasure. However, my teeth would still chatter, in counterpoint to my interior monologue.

I tried not to dwell on these difficulties for very long, but instead turned my attention to my usual rainy-season breakfast—coffee, scrambled eggs, bread, and papaya or pineapple—and my preparations for the morning. I dressed in a new peasant blouse and black skirt, trying to look especially festive, but not eccentric.

The blasting of the tape-recorded song continued as I walked out into the street, greeting my neighbors, who were also dressed more festively and seemed to be in a mood of celebration. I noticed that the streets were filling with strange cars from Guatemala City. This I had been told to expect, as the people who had migrated from Zaragoza all tried to come back for fiestas; it was a time for renewing friendships and family ties.

The city folk looked a bit stuffy—the men in their suits and fancy shirts, and the women in their new dresses and high heels—but they all seemed to mingle with friends and relatives. It felt festive; however, everyone became solemn as we entered the cathedral. The altar, ordinarily quite plain, was decorated in splashes of blue, draped material, which came flowing from the ceiling to the altar. There were bouquets of flowers and candles everywhere. "The Altar Guild has done the decorating," my fictive mother, Silvia, explained. The Altar Guild is the high-status female society in the town. The mayor's wife and several councilmen's wives are appointed by the priest to this esteemed guild. My mother told me of a woman who had been appointed, but then had been disgraced, as she was *indecente*. (This woman, a married woman, had apparently been seen alone with a local married man, and such behavior was unacceptable.) My mother shook her head and said, "She was a poor example for her daughters, and *una mujer indecente*."

"Will she ever be forgiven?" I had asked.

Silvia looked surprised at my question, "*No, ella fue indecente*." (She used a particular family of the verb *to be*, which told me the woman was considered *permanently* indecent.) I understood the gravity of the sanction against her. I recalled my fictive sister Victoria once warning me about letting a certain married Zaragoza man visit me independently, because this was not proper. She had said, "To keep your respect, you must always have me or my mother with you should Roberto come to visit you alone." Roberto was an extremely handsome man, who loved to play the part of *muy hombre* (the local term for macho) in the town. I kept my respect and never allowed him into my house alone; I knew that I, too, was to obey the town's rules about proper behavior.

Religious Ceremonies

As the mass began for the fiesta Corpus Christi, the choir started singing, and the priest gave a short sermon and the mass. I gave my usual twenty-five centavos (far more than the tithe of the average zaragozaño) as the collection basket was passed. I was becoming accustomed to the mass and could even sing the songs in harmony. Incense was burning, and frightfully big firecrackers exploded outside the cathedral doors. The smoke caused us to cough and rub our eyes, but it was part of the celebration—no one complained. We all exited the cathedral as the procession began.

The mayor and his wife came up to me and said, "We'd like you to walk with us." I knew it was considered an honor and so replied, "I would be honored to do so. Thank you." However, I was somewhat fearful that I might make some kind of cultural blunder. I watched what they did and then tried to do the same thing. The crowd of several hundred people followed, the priest leading the procession with a *tambor y rizar* (drummer and a flute player) walking beside him. All were solemn and respectful; there was neither laughing nor talking.

The altars in the *capillas* (chapels) within the four cantones were festively decorated with flowers, candles, and statues. The capilla with the best-decorated altar received a prize. We walked first to the cantón to the east, then to the north, the west, and finally the south, nearest the cemetery. Prayers were said by the priest at each capilla. Although I couldn't distinguish the roles of various men in this ceremony, I was aware of the various statuses of the cofradias. The cofradias are an integral part of the religious hierarchical social system. The stages within the cofradia in Zaragoza range from the top level, *caciques* (chiefs), followed next by *ricos de segunda* (seconds-in-command), *jornaleros* (laborers), *mendigos* (beggars), and at the bottom, if counted at all, are the *indigenas*, the Indians (Mendéz, 1967:173). Each status is achieved and maintained through donations to the church. The system was changing throughout Latin America, because as the local areas become modernized, people find that the hierarchical system hampers their achieving economic advancement. In many towns the cofradia has gradually changed into cooperatives, as it has in Patzún; in Zaragoza, the cofradia system remains intact. This system defines many social relationships, such as one's godparent or ideal marriage partner.

Many aspects of life in Zaragoza are controlled by deeply ingrained social structures such as the cofradia; however, even areas influenced by the cofradia are known to shift and change with time—marriage practices, for example. In years past, the people living within each cantón were (supposedly) related. The preferred marriage had been within one's own cantón. This endogamous system was to protect relatives from marrying outside bloodlines, and especially to protect from intermarriage with Indians. I had read old documents recording the amount of Indian blood each person carried. Each fraction of Indian blood made an individual less valued in that system.

However, by the time of my arrival in 1974 things had changed, and intermarriages between people from different cantones were allowed. Intermarriages between Indians and Ladinos were also permitted. Cultural rules and norms usually are adaptive: as the system changes, so do the rules. During the changing, people often have conflicting views of just what the rules are; most of them will simply say, "We don't pay attention to that nowadays." In both Zaragoza and Patzún fractions of blood are no longer recorded, a sign of a social change.

As with rules and norms, some of the symbols in a culture are covert and implicit: only through careful study, recording, and interpreting can one decode the meaning of them. Other symbols, however, are far more apparent, such as the decorations I saw around me during the procession with the priest, the mayor, and the townspeople. I found the symbols of the church most striking. The dirt streets were decorated in colored sawdust, which was the custom during celebrations. The ornamentation was simple but colorful—flowers and designs of doves, chalices, the cross, and other symbols of the Catholic church. The hours spent in creating the actual artwork were considered a form of penance. The drum and flute played mournfully, as we walked quietly, carrying a statue of the Virgin Mary. The figure was solemn, almost pitiful, dressed in a flowing gown of the traditional Virgin's colors (blue and white) and with a shawl covering her head. How like the women of Zaragoza, I thought, hidden and solemn.

Family Reunions and Celebrations

After the procession, the zaragozaños went to their homes to eat. I observed the compadrazgo system reflected in this occasion. Throughout Latin America, and especially in the rural, peasant communities, social relationships are formed around a system of co-parents; again, this system is based on religion. The Catholic ceremony of infant baptism created a ritual, fictive kinship system of parents, child, and co-parents. A *padre* (father) and *madre* (mother) choose co-parents (*padrino* and *madrina*) with various spiritual characteristics, such as integrity and faithfulness, and who also are of a higher social status, so that the parents have additional resources in raising their child. This system has great influence on the social relationships within the community, as the co-parents visit the child throughout his or her life, and the child, out of respect for the co-parents, also visits them frequently, often exchanging gifts.

In some families the godchild, *ahijado* or *ahijada*, is obligated to visit the co-parents every Sunday. Such an obligation sometimes requires long trips into other towns, but it is the custom! These customs and the system create a net of security for both the child and the co-parents. It is common for the *compadres* (co-parents) to share financially in the upbringing of the child. The godparents might help with educational expenses, for example, or they might pay for the celebration of a goddaughter's fifteenth birthday or for a marriage ceremony. Being a compadre is an honor, but it is also expensive.

Zaragozaños often eat with their compadres during the fiesta of Corpus Christi. Since I had no compadres, I ate with my fictive family. We enjoyed a simple meal of rice, tomatoes, and bread. They had neither a table nor chairs, so we stood around a counter and ate the food brought in by Antonia and Victoria, who had cooked it on an open fire on the patio. Then Silvia announced, "It is now time for a siesta, as we will have a late night. Why don't you rest in your house, and we'll come for you when it's time to go to the cofradia *celebración* in the home of Don Marquez." (Don Marquez is not related to my fictive family, even though he has the same name.)

"Don't I have to be invited by them?" I asked.

"Yes, people have to be invited, and we are inviting you," Mother said simply.

I went and rested. At about five o'clock, Victoria came to the door. "Are you ready to go to the celebración?" she asked. I could see that she had on a lovely blue dress with pink and blue flowers, the first time I had seen her in any color but black. She was beautiful.

"You look beautiful!" I exclaimed. "And yes, I'm ready for the party."

We walked several blocks to a home I'd never visited. Music was coming from the house, and as we approached, I could see the room was filled with people laughing, dancing, eating, and drinking—a party. As we entered I saw a box by the doorway, labeled *limosna* (donations). "Should I contribute?" I asked Victoria.

"Yes, if you want to," she answered. "A cofradia costs the family a lot of money—about $300 a year. The Marquezes will have the statue of the Virgin Mary for two years, and that is expensive."

I slipped in a quetzal, commenting as we entered the crowded room, "That's a lot of money. Why do families want to do that?"

"It gives you a good place in the community, and helps you work up to a higher rank in the cofradia. It's also good luck. Come see where they have put the statue of the Virgin Mary."

There in the corner of the living room was the statue that had been carried in the procession throughout the town that morning. "She will stay here for two years," Victoria said matter-of-factly. "Then she'll go to another home; she was in our home about three years ago, and we had good luck that year," she smiled, recalling.

The music was exciting. In one room was a group of mariachis dressed in black with silver-studded design, large silver belts, and large black, silver-decorated sombreros. They were handsome and flirtatious and they played fast Latin music. Some couples were dancing, but not many. This scene was very different from the dance I later attended in Patzún, where Indian women and men shuffled in a circle to the music of the marimba, the native instrument of Guatemala and southern Mexico.

"It's time for the singing." Victoria tugged on my arm, and we reentered the living room with its statue of the Virgin. The incense was lit, and the a capella singing began. The celebration was a mix between the secular (the Latin music) and the sacred (the hymn singing). Victoria had a strong soprano voice, and I began to harmonize as a second soprano. Others joined in; it was a memorable moment. Then, because there was so much smoke and incense, several people began coughing. Soon Victoria was coughing, and I quickly found that I was the only one singing—in my second soprano! With that everyone started laughing, and the solemn occasion came to an end. The music of the mariachis began again, and soon all the men—old and young alike—wanted to dance with la gringa. We danced a simple dance, and because it was so crowded it didn't last long. Since I hadn't eaten any food, I only sipped the drink—out of courtesy—but it was enough to know the beverage was the potent local liquor. (I assumed this was acceptable, since Victoria did the same thing.) Before long the crowd thinned, and Victoria said, "Now it's time for the ceremony." She looked excited, so I knew it would be an eventful experience for me.

The Queen from Los Angeles

The skies were clear as we walked to the plaza. In the gazebo, a local band began to play marches and patriotic songs. Approximately 300 people were now milling around. I noticed that women and children were present, a rare event in Zaragoza. The air was becoming electrified as the mayor and councilmen approached, accompanying a beautiful, young girl about eighteen years old. She was dressed in a formal white gown and wearing a small coronation crown.

"She's the Queen of the Day," Victoria explained. "I was the queen five years ago." Later Victoria showed me the photographs of herself in a beautiful white gown and wearing the decorated white crown. "It's an honor to be elected queen; the whole town votes. Only a pure girl [I assumed she meant a virgin] is chosen."

"I don't recognize that girl—who is she?" I asked.

"She's Olimpia Lucas, who lives in Los Angeles."

"What? She lives in Los Angeles?" I asked in a startled tone.

"Oh, that's not unusual," replied Victoria. "She is working there, and she sends money home to her parents. She is very brave, and the town is proud of her."

I could tell that Victoria agreed that Olimpia was brave and that perhaps she wanted to go to the United States, too. Later, we would talk about this dilemma, the pull to go to the States to earn money and the desire to stay home in Zaragoza. Victoria decided to stay in Guatemala.

"Will she ever return permanently?" I asked.

"Why, of course," answered Victoria. "This is her home." The pattern of migration is very common in Zaragoza, but not in Patzún, where few people leave town except to work temporarily in the harvest fields on the coast.

The crowning ceremony had now begun. It was long and repetitive; the speeches about the greatness of Zaragoza droned on and on. I heard bits and pieces about the battles the zaragozaños had fought and won with their neighbors surrounding them. One speaker told of the war in Patzicía, a town of Indians and Ladinos, five kilometers away. Only twenty years earlier (1954) a bloody battle had been fought in Patzicía over land rights. After the speeches the crowd began to sing the national anthem. I watched their faces and saw they were transformed, much as I have seen in the United States when "The Star-Spangled Banner" is sung. In Zaragoza, patriotism begins anew in each generation, and its value is renewed at each public assemblage.

Next came more firecrackers and music. The recessional began, ending that part of the celebration.

I Could Have Danced All Night

Now began the large, secular dance, to which all townspeople and out-of-towners were invited. The dance took place in part of the municipio building—in an empty rectangular area with folding chairs lined along the wall. A band consisting of a marimba, a bass violin, a bass drum, and a guitar played lively dance music in one corner. The charge to dance was only a few cents. I love to dance and could hardly wait to be asked to participate. My mother, Silvia, must have sensed my excitement. She looked at me with deadly serious eyes and issued a warning, "You must be very, very careful, not to dance with a 'bad man.' *Hay no decente hombres ahora* [There are no good men now]. Some men have been drinking, and they may not be good men tonight."

"How can I tell who is a bad man?" I asked simply.

"When a bad man asks you to dance, I will pull hard on your skirt, as a sign that you must say no. If I don't pull your skirt, you may dance with him."

"Thank you, Mother; I think that is a good plan," I answered.

I noticed that Antonía and her *novio* were dancing, but not too closely—Mother was watching. The rules of behavior for novios in Zaragoza are similar to those found in many Latin American cultures. A youth of about the age of eighteen may seek a steady relationship with one girl, his novia, who is usually a couple of years younger than he is. This dating period is considered a serious prenuptial arrangement. Although the couple proclaim their love, they are prohibited from having a sexual relationship. This restriction is to assure that the girl is a virgin on her wedding night and to protect the bloodlines of lineage. To ensure that this rule is obeyed, the couple is constantly supervised by a chaperone or the girl's parents. Of course, as in other societies, rules do get broken and bent. The social stigma associated with premarital sex and the alienation that occurs when one becomes pregnant were the greatest fears most teenage girls expressed to me. In Zaragoza a long and involved courtship, without sex, is supported through cultural expressions such as serenades (sometimes sung at the novia's window), flowery poetry, and gifts, all from the novio. The novia remains passive throughout the courtship. The rules I have described are especially expected of those in the upper classes.

Because my fictive family is considered upper class, Antonía and Victoria obeyed these cultural rules. Victoria and her novio had been dating for three years, but they had never been alone until they were married. They talked and kissed—sometimes for hours as they said goodnight on the front doorstep—always under the sharp eye of Silvia or Pablo, their father. This concern for chaperoning the young daughters was not as appreciable in Patzún—boys and girls were separated but without such strict attention.

"Mario is a man not to be trusted," my mother said, talking of Antonía's novio. "He's not a good man like Victoria's novio." Victoria's novio, Juan, was older, a businessman who traveled a couple of times a week to Nicaragua, selling and buying goods. I couldn't tell the difference between good and bad, but felt that Antonía's novio was very quiet and not as self-revealing as the boisterous novio of Victoria. Victoria and Juan planned to marry soon. Silvia and Pablo had bought a store for Victoria in Guatemala City in anticipation of her marriage. "We know that it is hard on a woman with a man on the road a lot, so we bought this store for her to run." Antonía's novio was building a modern house for her in Zaragoza, so I personally judged that he, too, was a decent man.

The music played, and I wanted to dance. Four or five men had asked me to dance, and with all of them I had received the strong jerk on my skirt, so I politely said, "No, gracias." I was beginning to think that there were no "good men" in Zaragoza, when the school principal, the man I had met my first day in Zaragoza, came and asked me to dance. What?! I didn't receive a pull on my skirt, so I danced with him.

On the dance floor I realized that all of the men were still wearing their sombreros, and the only women dancing were young señoritas. I noticed all the señoras were sitting and watching. I wondered if I had broken some social rule. Next the mayor of the town asked me to dance. No pull on my skirt, so we danced in a very dignified manner.

Before long I noticed that the señoras were gradually slipping out the door and that Silvia looked tired. "It's been a long day, Mother," I said. "I think it's time to go home."

"Yes, I agree," she said amiably.

We began to walk slowly to our homes. It was a dark, clear night, in spite of it being the rainy season. I marveled at the beauty of the night, the stars that hung so close to the surface of Earth, the happenings of the day, the warmth of renewals of friendships for so many. I said good night to Silvia and was soon in my bed. I could hear the beat of the marimba and the drum, and smiled at the lack of good men in Zaragoza.

A Test of Trust

Suddenly, at about four in the morning, the hair on the back of my neck began to rise. It was pitch dark in my bedroom, yet I knew that I was not alone. I could feel the "presence" of someone else. Then I saw the shadow of a figure slowly pass from the sidewalk outside my bedroom, beneath the doorway, and into my bedroom. The shadow passed slowly yet another time, and I could feel someone breathing heavily. A foot pushed against the bedroom door. Nothing. Quiet. All was quiet except my pounding heart. I could barely breathe. What to do?! I could hear his breathing, then again the pushing on my door. What to do?! I lay like a stone, my breath almost gone. Then I heard a "ping," and the light outside my living room door broke and went out. It was even darker now, and I felt trapped.

Next I heard him pushing on my front door, perhaps thinking it would be easier to break. The first time I inspected the house I had noticed how fragile the doors were. I knew I wasn't safe. I knew it would be only moments before the frail door would crash in. The only thing I could do was to *fight*. I leapt from my bed, rushed into the living room, and turned on the light. Next I yelled, "Get away! I'm not afraid of you!" I felt that my heart was going to burst from its pounding. The most bloodcurdling laughter came from the stranger on the other side. And, the pushing became harder—and harder—i could see the door begin to bulge. Time was running out. I just hoped the wood would hold. What to do?!

I opened my door to the patio and ran out into the courtyard. The night was quiet, dark. I tried to call out to my neighbors. I opened my mouth—it was as dry as cotton—and tried to squeak out a sound. Nothing came, only panic. I tried again. Still not even a little squeak. I shut my eyes and forced all I could—at last a shout came out of my throat and into the night. "Help me, help me! Neighbors. A thief is at my door! [I didn't know the Spanish word for *killer* or *rapist*, although such possible outcomes raced through my mind.] Help me! Help me!" Quiet. Not a sound, not a light. The cotton in my mouth again took over. I flashed back to the day I had visited Professor Mendéz at the University of San Carlos in Guatemala City to discuss with him my plans to do my fieldwork in Zaragoza. He was encouraging, but he had warned, "If you ever need help, you won't find any in that town. The zaragozaños are very individualistic, competitive, and protective of their own." Now I thought I was to be shown the lesson that the gringa was on her own! But I knew that I would go down fighting. I had that streak of fight in me!

I reentered my living room. The door was still holding, but the pounding was becoming harder and harder—a thud and a crack sounded with each blow. I picked up my broom and shouted bravely at the intruder, "Get out of here; I'm armed. I have a gun and I'm not afraid to shoot! Come through this door and you're a dead man!" I was pretty brave for one who didn't believe in guns and who had never held one in her hand.

The memory of Magdelena in Xajáxac holding the machete the night we had heard of the killings in the highlands came back to me and reinforced my bravery. Then I began to hear other noises—

the voices of my neighbors—twenty to thirty of them, running with brooms and pitchforks and sticks. They had indeed heard my cries for help. And they had come to save me. They cared! My mother put her arms around me and said, "I will not leave; I will sleep beside your bed." And so she slept in my doorway the whole night. They never found the man who had been trying to break into my house; Silvia excused the men of Zaragoza by saying, "It must have been a stranger passing through."

The next day she declared, "I'm moving in with you."

"No, please, Mother, I need to be alone to do my work at night [as I would type my fieldnotes long after everyone had turned out their lights and hopped into their ponchos]. But I want to thank you and all the people from Zaragoza for coming to my aid. What should I do?"

"You should have a mass said for the people of Zaragoza, for their good luck. You should have a big mass said," Mother answered confidently. And I did. The next Sunday, I paid twenty-five dollars for the best mass that could be said; there were flowers at the altar, candles, fireworks, and even a choir. And best of all, the priest said a special prayer from "the woman from the United States to thank the people of Zaragoza for their kindness." I never had another incident like this during my time in Zaragoza. It was in later reflection that I realized what a test of faith this incident had been. Although I didn't know the words to describe my situation and I didn't know my intruder or all of the rescuers, help came. I deeply hope this basic human instinct will not be extinguished in our present-day violent society but will remain a universal value of reaching out and helping other humans in distress.

Chapter 9

Seeing the Separate Systems in a Culture

It is in the analysis of the way in which a system operates within a whole culture that exposes its relative importance. Separate systems of a culture should move harmoniously, for it is system discord or asynchrony that impels change.
—Margarita Kay, *The Anthropology of Human Birth*, 1982

The incident with the intruder began to drift into the past. Settling into my home in Zaragoza and staying often in my room with the Maczuls in Patzún filled my first months of fieldwork. Semana Santa (Holy Week) passed, and the urgency of another spring, planting crops, and waiting for the monsoonal rains occupied the daily lives of the people. *Most* fieldwork is simple day-to-day activities, such as helping to feed the family or preparing the fields. Not every day is filled with excitement and fiestas; much is simply doing what needs to be done. However, it is the job of the anthropologist to maintain a sharp, discerning eye, to probe and study patterns in all of the ordinary things that need to be done. It is through analyzing these ordinary activities and events that the whole of a culture begins to emerge and the patterns that form the various systems of the culture are revealed.

Just Doing the Things That Need to Be Done

I found the rhythm of life in both Zaragoza and Patzún to my liking. On a typical morning in Patzún, the neighborhood roosters gathered up their steam long before daylight, and the cow next door stood ready to fill my enameled cup with warm milk, thanks to the courtesy of my neighbor. I learned to wash and scrub my clothes (how I hated to wash the bedsheets) in my private pila and spread the wet items on the grass beside it to dry. I had washed my clothes just once in the public pila in Patzún and found it was difficult to carry items back and forth in a woven basket—I had wished I could learn to carry the basket on my head as the Indians did. I had also tried to get my water from the central water fountain in Patzún as all of the other women did. It wasn't as easy as it first looked; the long bamboo cane needs to be placed just right into one of the spouts, and the narrow-necked water jug must be held steady as it fills with water. The Indian women gracefully fill their jugs; then they place the jugs on their heads and walk nimbly down rutted pathways and up many hills, back to their homes, without spilling a drop. Even if I filled mine half-full, it was still too heavy to manage with both hands. Several women had tried to teach me to carry the jug on my head, but I soon realized, and they too (after much laughter) that my head was just too old to teach new tricks.

Since I didn't make my own tortillas, I wasn't obligated to go to the *molinar* (the mill plant where corn is ground into masa) with the other women in either town. But I joined their long lines anyway, just to talk and watch them. So much of a highland woman's time is spent on simple tasks, such as getting corn ground, making tortillas, gathering wood, washing clothes in the pila, and walking to the outdoor market for a day's supply of tomatoes, potatoes and rice. In the first few months of my fieldwork I learned just how labor-intensive and -extensive are the lives of women in the towns. I didn't have to weave cloth for the family, raise chickens and pigs, or help the male family members plant the corn and harvest, yet these are the things the highland women do, day in and day out. Since all cooking is done on an open fire (except the Andrade's, which will be described later), dry wood needs to be gathered daily. Thus, women and small children walk farther and farther each day searching for firewood, which takes more and more of their time.

Basic Nutrition: A Universal Human Need

When ethnographers study cultures, they investigate all aspects of peoples' lives. One important aspect is health. Rules and norms about family and childbirth are of little importance if women don't have sufficient nutrients to be fertile or to carry a baby to full term.

A sanitary—but difficult—way to get water

Without strong bodies, men would have difficult lives as hoe-and-machete farmers or laborers in Guatemala City. Nutrition is an important aspect of a culture, and an anthropologist must investigate, to learn how adaptive it is for the culture.

The staple foods of Zaragoza and Patzún are boiled black beans, rice, and tortillas. In both towns, these same staple foods are eaten three times a day throughout the year. The people with higher incomes also add a simple vegetable soup (cooked with a small amount of meat) to their daily diets. Occasionally, zaragozaños and patzuñeros supplement their meals with dried fish, used especially for flavor. During the rainy season, papayas, melons, and pineapples are brought up from the coastal areas and can be bought at reasonable prices. Bananas and tomatoes are available all year long, also at reasonable prices. Limes grow wild in some areas, providing much-needed vitamin C.

Milk and other dairy products are scarce in both towns; my neighbor in Zaragoza had the only dairy cow in town. How do the people get enough calcium and vitamin D in their diets? I wondered. Calcium is essential to many of the body's functions. Are the people of the highlands deficient in calcium? There was no way I could judge their conditions except by just looking at them. I have written in earlier chapters that the people who first settled this area, the ancestors of the Maya, had crossed from Asia into North America about 25,000 years ago. Lactose intolerance (difficulty digesting milk products) is a prevalent condition among people of Oriental descent, and thus, I assume that some of the zaragozaños and patzuñeros, perhaps even a majority, are lactose intolerant. This inherited intolerance for milk products causes gastrointestinal problems. After observing more closely the quantity and types of food the local people ate, I began to believe that their diet was adequate in supplying calcium and vitamin D. Their high consumption of beans and tortillas most likely provided a sufficient amount of calcium. Later, a nutritionist told me (personal communication) that the local diet does provide an adequate amount of calcium and vitamin D; however, the amount of calories is insufficient for adequate metabolism. It is this lack of calories that causes malnutrition.

Work Roles of Women: Labor Intensive and Labor Extensive

Women are not only in charge of overseeing the healthful nutrition of their families, but they also are in charge of preparing food for the large kin groups gathered at celebrations, such as baptisms, weddings, and birthdays. Celebrations are very much a part of keeping social networks intact, but they take a tremendous amount of women's labor. One of my neighbors in Patzún was the grandmother of more than twenty-five grandchildren, all of whom lived near or actually in the compound household. The courtyard of the compound house looked like a kindergarten, with so many children running around.

One day I was helping this grandmother prepare a *pastilla de cumpleaños* (birthday cake) (I mixed the batter in a large bowl with a fork). "I wish there weren't so many birthdays," she laughingly commented. "We have to make a cake every week—there are over fifty living here in this house!" I gasped, thinking about the labor that went into feeding, clothing, cleaning, and washing for this family.

Mothers and daughters are the workforce behind the daily household chores. Young daughters begin helping to fetch water by the age of three or four; by the age of seven, they are busy at such work as washing clothes and gathering wood. In Patzún, girls

Laughter and sharing—part of the Indian lifestyle

learn to weave and embroider by the age of nine. During the harvest, they carry food to the fields and help their mothers store the corn as it is brought back from the fields (they keep the corn in buildings located in the family compound). Seldom did I see children sitting and playing, except on the weekends.

Seeing the Finer Differences

In both Zaragoza and Patzún, couples marry and start families at early ages; as each new generation approaches the ages of eighteen to twenty-two, they perpetuate the preceding cycle. Childhood is short, and maybe sweet, but certainly linked with the household economy and maintaining family ties. The rhythm of life, from sunrise to sunset, at first seems peaceful and simple in these highland towns; however, the first encounter with a new culture is often deluding, as the details and differences are sometimes masked behind all the newness. Slowly one's senses begin to adjust and to categorize patterns of behaviors, revealing a far more complex lifeway than originally thought.

An important part of cultural studies is observing the physical features of the people. Physical features help an anthropologist form hypotheses about the origins of the people being studied, perhaps about their migration patterns, and also about their mating patterns. Understanding the laws of inheritance is critical when one studies a population and its ability to adapt to a specific ecological niche. For instance, the people living in the rain forests of Brazil have different physical features than the Eskimos of Greenland or the businesspeople on Wall Street. My training in physical anthropology helped me to uncover some interesting patterns of physical difference between the townspeople of Zaragoza and the townspeople of Patzún. The first and most obvious difference is that many zaragozaños look Caucasian, like the gypsies featured in photographs of southern Europe. Some have blond hair and blue eyes—though the majority have dark brown hair and brown eyes—and children under five years are often blond. Also, almost every person from Zaragoza has curly hair and dimples, in contrast to the coarse, black, straight hair of the men and women of Patzún. The most striking difference between the two groups is stature. Several women in Zaragoza are as tall as I—five-feet-nine—and, according to Euro-American standards, many are average height. The patzuñeros are well proportioned but shorter than an average Euro-American; in fact, they are considered among the shortest people in the world. Padre Sergio, the Catholic priest in Patzún,

*Neighbor children in
Zaragoza (notice the blond
hair of the little Ladina)*

would always comment that he could see my head far above the 400 to 500 Indian heads at mass.

Dress is probably the next most obvious difference between the two groups of people. Watching my *Ladina* neighbors, I found that older women with children almost universally wore a loose-fitting, gray or black—occasionally pastel pink or blue—cotton dress with a dirty apron and a black shawl around their shoulders and heads. I had never seen any of them in something bright—no reds or yellows, only a dull gray or black. Might the color be symbolic of their lives? Reflective of their values? Younger girls and women of Zaragoza wear black slacks and white, gray, or black blouses. Again, I seldom saw a bright color worn by children or young women. What does color symbolize in a culture?

In contrast to the dull colors worn by the women of Zaragoza, the flash of color worn by both the men and women of Patzún is almost blinding. Small boys and girls are dressed alike in Patzún's traditional colors of red and blue until they are about three years of age. Boys then wear trousers with a colorful, hand-woven shirt, and girls wear bright-red blouses embroidered with blue, white, and yellow flowers, and bright-blue striped skirts. Older men and women wear the same colors as the children. The clothes worn by the patzuñeros appear still brighter against their brown adobe houses, which blend into the sides of the surrounding hills. The stark contrast of color in the two towns is a cultural artifact; it reflects their different lifestyles.

In both towns the men and women walk barefoot much of the time, or they wear the heavy sandals made from discarded automobile tires that I mentioned earlier. In Zaragoza the younger women sometimes wear plastic sandals. Generally, the feet of zaragozaños and patzuñeros are leathery and thick soled from walking without shoes. I described the adaptive quality of going barefoot in my account of my first days in Chimaltenango. During my 1974 fieldwork I confirmed that bare feet are more adaptive than stiff leather shoes in this type of setting. In the rainy season my leather shoes became moldy very quickly. They were not adaptive.

Receptions and Reflections

Bit by bit the differences emerged between the two towns. I kept wanting to ask more questions, but I knew that the people needed to get to know me better and learn that they could trust me. The first week I had been in Zaragoza, the mayor and three town councilmen visited me. I was surprised to see them, but I quickly invited them in and offered them a seat.

"Would you like some coffee?" I asked.

"No," the mayor replied. "We have come to ask you some questions about why you are here."

I was a little surprised at the directness of the question; however, I thought they seemed only curious—not threatening. "I'll be glad to tell you," I responded. "But are you sure you don't want some coffee and cookies? I have some made."

"Oh, gracias, Señora, you are very kind," they all replied, smiling. This seemed to relax us all. As I scurried into my kitchen, leaving them to look at my decorated living room, I recalled Silvia's first response to my house, "Why did you paint your walls such a dull white color? And why didn't you put some pictures of saints on the walls?" I had hoped theirs would be different.

As we sat drinking the coffee and eating the cookies, I began my explanation. "I bring you greetings from the headmaster of the university where I am a student." I brought out the letter with the letterhead of the University of Colorado on it—written in Spanish and signed by the chair of the Department of Anthropology—which stated that I was a bona fide student and that my research was legitimate and asked for "safe passage" for me. I could tell that the mayor was impressed. Each councilman read the letter and smiled. I was glad my dissertation director, Waldemar Smith, had suggested that I carry such a document.

"I am a mother and want to learn how mothers in your town care for their children and how they plan what size family is best to have." I tried to be accurate, while phrasing my plans in a way that would be acceptable and understood by the men and women of Zaragoza alike. Their faces looked blank. Perhaps they didn't understand.

I continued, "I hope to learn things by just staying with you here, living as you do, for about a year. Then I will write a book about what I have learned, and I will send you a copy to put in the municipal building."

With that, they all began to smile, and the mayor said, "That would be very, very nice, to have a book about us here in Zaragoza, gracias."

(Indeed I did write a book about them, my dissertation, and sent a bright-red bound copy to my fictive parents, who gave it to the mayor. Silvia said it sits on the mayor's desk. I had tried to get my dissertation published in Spanish but found the cost prohibitive at the time. Even though it is written in English, the townspeople treasure the photographs of them and of the buildings of Zaragoza.)

The men left shortly, but every day or so, I would walk by the municipal building and give greetings to the mayor, the clerks, and the councilmen. When there were special ceremonies, the mayor would introduce me—and my husband and children, if they were there—to the crowd gathered and would sometimes ask us to walk beside him and his wife during public parades.

When I first moved into my room in Patzún, I went to the mayor's office and explained my work to him and also showed him the letter from the department head. Even though he and the town clerk were pleasant, they seemed indifferent toward my presence in Patzún. Perhaps because I lived with a prominent Indian family, they felt my work was legitimate, or perhaps it was unimportant in their daily, busy lives. Also a gringa was not at all unusual in Patzún, since American nuns lived there and thousands of European and American tourists passed through the town on the way to Lake

Atitlán. I never had the opportunity to stand beside the Patzún mayor—perhaps that gesture wasn't deemed necessary in a town of Indian power. In Zaragoza, on the other hand, the people seemed very self-conscious about being disliked by the outside world, so any show of affection and concern was seen as a personal victory for the town. Some zaragozaños would ask me, "Do you like us better than the people in Patzún?" This caused me to reflect upon *my own* feelings of being accepted, rejected, ignored, threatened or whatever, as these feelings are also an important part of the fieldnotes. These personal reflections helped me to understand my own value system and also the value systems of the two cultures I was studying.

Days and weeks went by; I had much to do, but I could feel the trust growing between me and the others. In both towns I began a household survey of pregnancy histories (discussed later) and hired interviewers from each town to help out. People greeted me in both towns, and children in Zaragoza would play by my window. I had invited my fictive family in Zaragoza to my home for several meals, and occasionally, I would be invited to someone's home for a celebration of a birthday or a christening. On some evenings the zaragozaños' strolling guitar players would stop by my house and serenade me at my window. In Patzún, the older daughter of the family invited me on several outings. I could tell the townspeople were beginning to trust me.

Chapter 10

Coping through Competition and Rigid Rules
The Ladino Family

Among the members of the human race there exists an extra-ordinary variability in the breadth and sophistication of our understanding of what life is all about.
—M. Scott Peck, *The Road Less Traveled*, 1978

Family, a universal social unit, is the vehicle, the means through which cultural learning takes place. Here children are taught cultural norms, values, rules, and practices; here they adopt the features of the culture into which they were born and assimilate into mainstream society. Throughout this ethnography I have emphasized this unit, the family, as key to learning a culture. My fictive family in Zaragoza had become the central force in my fieldwork life. My compound family in Patzún was beginning to help me learn the Indian culture. I was learning two separate lifeways simultaneously.

It wasn't long after beginning the fieldwork that I could distinguish various types of families in each town—there is a culture of families with distinct rules and norms for each social stratum. Though the towns are agricultural and economically poor, this does not mean that there is only one social status. The range of incomes isn't as great as can be found in complex urban centers, but social variations still exist. In Zaragoza there are also occupational

109

variations—not all of the families in Zaragoza are hoe-and-machete farmers.

Uncovering the variations within the two cultures led me to look more carefully at the roles of men. Men in the two towns are quite different, not only in physical appearance, as I have already described, but also in the ways in which they act toward and relate to women.

What Happens in a Town without Men?

In Zaragoza men have a particular rhythm to their work, and they relate differently to their wives and other females than they do to one another. For instance, I noticed that at about four o'clock every Monday morning, a large crowd of approximately 100 men assembled in the plaza, boarding buses heading for the capital. At first I thought that it was just a day trip, perhaps for a special job. But after observing a couple of Mondays, I realized that the men didn't return at night, or for the rest of the week. In fact, the town was almost deserted of adult men during the week.

"Why do all the men go to town and not return for a week or so?" I asked several women neighbors.

"They work in the City, doing all kinds of jobs," the women replied. "They work to bring us some cash; zaragozaños, our men, aren't good farmers, so they need to do other kinds of work. Their hearts aren't in farming."

"But isn't that expensive, to have two homes? One in the City and one here?" I asked naively.

"Some of the men live in one room all together; they sleep there and eat in the streets. Others have other wives and families in the City. The other wives *aren't their real wives*, because I'm the *first wife* and have all the inheritance, but the other women take care of them, feed them, and give them a room to live in."

"And the children. Who provides for the children?" I asked.

"The other woman gets her share of help, but mine are the *real* children."

"The real children?"

"Yes, my children are the real ones, the ones who get the inheritance." I now understood the differences within the family hierarchy and how inheritance is determined. The married women living in Zaragoza really did have implicit power—that of controlling the inheritance.

"Aren't you jealous of the other woman?" I asked the zaragozañas directly.

"Oh, yes, we don't like it at all, but that is the way of the man, to be muy hombre. And a woman is supposed to suffer—we are like the Virgin Mary." The Ladina had described the role expectations of both men and women and the meaning of the *machismo complex* and the *marianismo* or *madonna cult*. Many Latin American authorities have analyzed these phenomena; some feel the macho complex is due to a feeling of insecurity and inferiority, as Octavio Giraldo (1972) says (my translation):

> To a Mexican friend you may criticize his country and perhaps get away with it; you may talk to him of bribery, corruption, politics and religion and he still may not take offense. But if you question his manhood, if you belittle his ability to make love, if you even hint at impotence, you not only have an enemy, you may get a knife in your back. They take their love life and themselves that seriously. It is their Achilles heel. (98)

Giraldo believes the perfect counterpart to the macho complex is the madonna cult, that of the ideal submissive, virginal woman. The unpardonable offense is for a groom to find his bride is not a virgin. It threatens his manhood, for his bride may be more passionate than he (Giraldo, 1972:306). The madonna cult idealizes the woman by making her a saint in her own home, a mistress of her four walls, and a slave to her man. The man then compliments—and is a complement to—the ideal mother and wife, who is on a pedestal, removed from sexual desires and needs.

In some societies, a psychological desire for children is bound with the need to demonstrate machismo. Offspring supply proof of a male's potency, and a male child in particular is considered evidence that a man has sexual powers. (Perhaps this sounds unusual, but traces of the machismo complex can be found in the United States, as when a son is the preferred first child.) My theory of machismo is socioeconomic. In uncovering the complementary sexual roles in the everyday lives of men and women in both towns, I found that a simple psychological theory was insufficient to explain the complexity of the interacting sexual roles. The socioeconomic theory came to light as I explored further the pattern of recurrent migration of the males in Zaragoza.

"But while your men are away, aren't they worried that you might find other men, too?"

The women laughed and replied, "Who would we find in Zaragoza?"

Looking around at the empty streets and at the stray older men and very young boys, I realized that they were right. Over half of the men of Zaragoza had migrated to the City to return two weeks

Zaragoza women and children, somber and withdrawn

later. Perhaps this absence accounted for the poorly groomed appearance of the women; they seemed perpetually depressed, and poor grooming is one sign of depression. I knew there was sufficient water in the town, but the women tended to be grimy and ill kept.

I asked a leading question: "How do you tolerate not having men around Zaragoza?"

"Our men forbid us to leave our homes except to get a few supplies at the store and to have our corn ground at the molinar. They would hit us if they learned that we have been visiting and gossiping." (I believe this was a threat and not a decision carried out often. During my fieldwork, I heard of only one woman being beaten, an incident to which the townspeople objected strongly.) "After you marry, you are to stay behind the walls of your home;

it's safer that way."

This explanation helped me to understand why the town's pila was dry, and also why I never saw a woman on the street alone or visiting with other women. This sanction and rule also helped to explain why the townspeople had turned down having a central pila built for women to do their daily wash—and also perhaps to gossip. Instead water is piped into their homes. Thus, their privacy forces the protection of their reputations.

The men's absence from the town also leaves it with strong internal sanctions to control the behavior of all. Each woman is isolated behind her own wall; there are no cooperatives or mother's clubs such as I found in Patzún. I learned from the nuns and schoolteachers that several attempts to create such groups had been made, but each effort had failed, because the women were not allowed—or didn't allow themselves—to participate in group activities outside their homes.

The consequences of this social organization are widely felt. The women, alone in their homes, have no mutual support. This organization also prevents women from producing any income through cottage industries, such as in Patzún where the Indian women are always weaving or embroidering items to sell to tourists, free to do so.

A Family Protects Its Inheritance

I began to uncover systematically the lives of the women in Zaragoza by focusing on three classes of women: upper, middle, and lower. I began with a middle-income person, one with a large family. I was sitting with my neighbor, Isabela, one afternoon, having a cup of coffee, when I heard her describe her life as one of sorrow. "Like the Virgin Mary, I have suffered," she said. "I met Miguel when I was twenty years old. He was twenty-five and had already lived with another woman on the coast for three years; they had had three children. She wasn't good for him, he said, so we moved in together. We've been together for forty-four years and during this time Miguel has lived with six other women. I don't know how many children he has, and I don't care as I have the only real children." Again I learned that women have power through their children and the inheritance pattern.

"Life is not easy for a woman," she continued, staring vacantly at the pink-painted wall covered with religious calendars and family portraits. The cement floor was clean, but empty. Only a few straight-backed chairs and a wardrobe with a mirror constituted the furniture in the living room. A doorway led to an open courtyard flourishing with subtropical flowers and blossoming fruit trees. A few ducks, chickens, and turkeys cackled and gobbled their disapproval of being penned in one corner of the yard.

"Ten of our thirteen children are still living. Three boys died in infancy of bronchopneumonia."

An eighteen-year-old daughter was washing the family clothes at the pila centered in the courtyard. She was Juanita, youngest of the thirteen children. By all standards she was very pretty, with dark curly hair and dimpled cheeks. Her dress was wrinkled and gray. Another sister, Marta, wore a dark polyester pantsuit. She was not as pretty, but perhaps more intelligent. Marta was studying English at a private school in Guatemala City; she planned to become a bilingual secretary and to work in the City. Marta lived with a brother and his family in Guatemala City, but she returned often to Zaragoza, because she didn't like the noise and smog of the capital.

"Our children all have gone to school, but neither my husband nor I have. Miguel can sign his name, but I can't even do that," Isabela explained. She then described each one of her ten living children and their families. I knew she was proud of them. "None of my daughters works outside the home; it's better that way," she continued. "Our oldest son lives right here in Zaragoza and farms the family land; he has eight children and wants more."

"What does having a big family mean to you, Isabela?" I asked.

"I think that it is God's will. A woman should have as many children as possible." Her daughter, the eighteen-year-old, called out, "Nowadays they cost too much." She added, "I don't want to get married until I'm at least twenty-five years old, and maybe not even then." Changing generational norms, I thought.

Isabela recalled vividly the years of raising ten children. She had neither relatives nor a hired maid. She preferred this to living with her in-laws, because "mothers-in-law can be very mean." At about five years of age, a daughter begins to help care for other siblings and to run errands; by eight years she assists with the cooking and washing clothes. Boys from middle-income families begin going to the fields with their fathers when they are about four years old, "just to watch." By about age seven, they are helping to hoe the fields and carry cargo of various sorts.

"But you know the zaragozaños are not good farmers; they don't like the work. They go to the capital to make money and come home on the weekends to work in the fields." I had heard this explanation several times, and I wasn't certain whether the comment was to justify or to challenge their work habits. By working the land only part-time, zaragozaños aren't as successful in farming as the patzuñeros are—who work in the City for wages only occasionally.

"When it is time to harvest, all my sons and their sons come to do the work. Sometimes we need to hire a few people, but most of the time we do all of the work ourselves." My conversation with Isabela helped me to link the reasons that zaragozaños continue to have many children (as a workforce during the harvest times) with the concept of a total support system. For instance, Marta, the older daughter, lived with her brother in the City, and most likely paid very little or no rent; thus, her family served as an economic support system.

"Do your daughters have it easier than you did?" I asked.

"I think it's about the same. When I was young, I did all of my own work, but I stayed home. Most of my daughters left Zaragoza when they were about fifteen years of age to work in Guatemala City as muchachas." This practice means that daughters are early producers of wages as maids. After a Ladino woman marries, however, she is in control of the household economy through her own and her children's powers of inheritance only. In Patzún the opposite is true. The Indian women are continuous producers and sharers in the household economic welfare, but they receive no inheritance except by their association to (and the goodwill of) their sons.

Isabela's grayed hair; slumped, thin body; and wrinkled, dirty dress disguised the pretty woman she probably once was. As a señorita, dancing had been her greatest joy, she told me; however, this time of life is short in Zaragoza. "Dances are for señoritas." (I wonder if perhaps this explained why someone had tried to break into my house the night of the dance, as I, a señora, had broken the rule for dancing.) The goal of life for Isabela was for her children and grandchildren to respect her. Respect is an important principle in Zaragoza culture. Rarely is a señora to be seen in the streets, "if she is respectable," and then only with another señora, and husbands are seldom seen in public with their wives. This practice is unlike the tradition in Patzún, where the family goes many places together and are often seen touching each other. In Zaragoza, even in church, men and women sit on opposite sides of the aisle— women on the left, the heart side, I was told.

"I am wife number one," Isabela told me, again. "All of my children—and none of my husband's other children—will share in the inheritance . . . both my sons and daughters equally. But because we don't have much land, they will probably keep it all as one, and Alberto [the eldest] will continue to farm it. We have a horse to carry things; most people don't have one, but we worked hard for it. My sons and grandsons are hard workers. They are my life now that I am old."

A Family Moving Up

Isabela's description of her life and her family is, I found, very typical of her generation of middle-income families. I also studied the upper- and lower-income groups in Zaragoza and Patzún. The Andradé family is an example of an upper-income family in Zaragoza—a family moving up. Carmen was thirty-four years old and a schoolteacher at the time I interviewed her. Her husband, Humberto, thirty-five years old, worked as a city clerk. Both of them had completed the equivalent of a high-school education in Chimaltenango. They had three children, and all five members of the Andradé family lived with Carmen's widowed mother, who also cared for the children while Carmen and Humberto worked.

The Andradé home was larger than most in Zaragoza; it had two bedrooms—most homes had only one. It also had a porcelain flush toilet (I didn't have one) and a cold-water shower. They owned a modern television set, a vinyl-covered sofa and vinyl-covered chairs, and a stereophonic record player. Cooking was done in the kitchen on a wood-burning stove (it was the only other stove in Zaragoza besides the one in my home). The only wall decoration was a picture of the current president of the Republic; there were no pictures of saints or of the Virgin Mary.

Several reasons for the Andradé family's greater wealth were apparent. Humberto had inherited some land from his deceased parents and, since he didn't like to farm, rented it out to an Indian for four quetzales a month and a percentage of the crop grown on it. Also, both husband and wife were salaried employees. Carmen was on birth control pills, because they did not want more children. The Andradés had high expectations for their children. "We want our children to have a good education, maybe even to become doctors and lawyers. Our families are all getting better educations, and we're improving our way of life."

Carmen, attractive in her white blouse and dark-green skirt, remarked, "We see Zaragoza as our home, but we don't really live here." Humberto commented further, "Most of our friends live in Antigua or Chimaltenango. We plan to keep on living here, as it is less expensive to live here than in the other towns."

The Poorest-of-the-Poor

On the other end of the continuum was the Hernández family. Jorge and Tina had been living together since Tina was sixteen and Jorge was twenty-four years old. They lived in a cane hut in a gully on the outskirts of Zaragoza. Jorge had lived with another woman before he met Tina and had had three children with her, but he did not support them and hadn't seen them for twelve years. Jorge was thirty-six years old when I interviewed him, but he looked much older to me; his fat, round face was pasty-white, and all of his teeth were missing. "The doctor at the clinic says I have thin blood," Jorge said flatly.

Tina was pregnant again. She and Jorge already had five children who ranged in age from six months to ten years. She had had two stillbirths and two miscarriages before the sixth month of her current pregnancy. My calculations were that Tina and Jorge had been together for twelve years, so she must have gotten pregnant almost every year. At twenty-eight years of age, her hair was thin, and she, too, was toothless. Jorge never attended school, and Tina had gone for only one year. "We can't read or write; it's bad to have to sign with your thumbprint and not to know what the signs say." Not one of their six children was attending school: "We have to work," Jorge said emphatically.

I came to their cane hut often to buy eggs (they owned two chickens). I would pay them ten cents for every egg I bought. I often paid them before receiving an actual egg (just in case the hen laid one that day), knowing that they needed the cash and that pride kept them from begging. Many times I asked them to eat "my" egg, saying I was on a diet.

After getting to know the family, I asked Tina if I could spend one day and night with the family, just so that I could understand their lives better. At first Tina seemed to think I was joking, but when I told her that I would pay her fifteen quetzales for her kindness, she grew excited and said she would ask Jorge. That night I heard a knock on the door and found Tina and three of her children there. "Jorge says it would be good to have you come and stay with us," Tina said.

"Good, thank you," I replied. "How about tomorrow?"

"That's OK."

I commented that I would bring my sleeping bag, so that I wouldn't have to bother them for a poncho, and that I needed to drink special water, so I would bring my own jug. "Otherwise," I explained, "I will do what you do and eat what you eat." I then paid Tina the fifteen quetzales.

The next morning I told Silvia that I would not be staying at home that night and that I would stay with the Hernández family. "Be careful. They're not to be trusted," she cautioned. (Zaragozaños often issue a caution to reassure that statuses are maintained. This occurred in many similar situations.)

Tina was washing clothes in a bucket of water when I arrived; it was about midmorning. I sat on an old bench outside their cane hut, talking with Tina. The baby, Miguel, was lying on a shelf propped up by plastic buckets with a mosquito net over his body. (Ladino women do not use rebozos to keep their babies on their backs as the Indian mothers do.) Flies were everywhere, as the Hernández house was near a stream that flowed around the perimeter of Zaragoza. Tina's work seemed tedious, but with both hands free, she completed the job quickly.

When Tina breastfed Miguel, she sat on the ground or on the bench and focused only on feeding him; she didn't attempt to do handiwork or anything else with her hands during that time. I knew I was observing a learned pattern of behavior, a pattern taught to young girls as they observe their mothers and which had been passed down through many generations. It is imperative that a fieldworker analyze these micro events in the lives of the women being studied, because such analysis tells the complex story of women and of their roles and statuses in the family and in the society. The ethnographer should not evaluate whether these ways are better or worse than other such cultural patterns; they are simply norms that are a part of that society. At the same time, the interpretation must be within the *context* of what the fieldworker has learned about a particular culture: Does the behavior amount to any difference in the productivity of the women? Does it change anything about their reproduction?

After observing Tina, I noticed that all zaragozañas carry their infants in front of them, rather than in a rebozo on their backs, like the patzuñeras. When I asked several women from Zaragoza about this practice, they replied, "If we'd carry our babies on our backs we'd look like Indians." And when I asked women from Patzún why they don't carry their babies in front of them, they responded by saying, "We couldn't do any work that way." These differences in child rearing illustrate some of the differences in the cultural values of work and productivity.

Tina interrupted her washing to invite me into the house. The cane hut was eight-by-ten feet, with an earthen floor. One area was separated for cooking over an open fire on the floor, although Tina also cooked outdoors. The sleeping area consisted of four grass mats. The latrine was located beside the house. The hut did not

Tina Hernández, Zaragoza mother, with infant Miguel (note her manner of carrying the baby)

contain electricity or potable water. During the rainy season the stream behind the Hernández house overflowed with muddy water and soaked the surrounding area.

The Hernández children appeared dispirited. Their faces were covered with dirt and sores, and their bellies were bloated, probably with worms, because of inadequate nutrition. "One is always sick," Tina complained, "and the druggist bills are so high." Her face lightened up as she showed me a bag of Incaparina (the local high-protein drink) that the new female doctor at the public health clinic had given her that morning.

Tina had some hot water boiling on the open fire and poured some into a large plastic cup; then she handed me a jar of instant coffee. I added a spoonful of coffee to the water and asked her if she wanted some. "No, not right now," she replied. We sat on the grass mats and talked about what she and the children were planning on doing the rest of the day.

"What do Jorge and your sons do during the day?" I asked.

"Jorge, Juan [ten years old], and Franco [eight] get up at about four in the morning; they eat the beans and tortillas that I prepare the night before; then they walk about two kilometers to work in the fields. They carry water, beans, and tortillas with them and eat at about noon. Jorge does the heaviest work with the bigger hoe, but the boys are strong and help, too. I wish they could go to school, but we need their help. The patron pays Jorge ten quetzales a month, and the boys each earn about two quetzales; sometimes the patron forgets to pay us."

I calculated the figures and said, "That's about 168 quetzales a year." (Remember the family that spent 300 quetzales in order to have the statue of the Virgin in their home for a year. This gives some comparison of income and use of resources.) I asked, "Do you earn anything?"

"No, I wish I could, but what can I do? When the girls are older, maybe fourteen, they can work as muchachas in the capital or down on the coast."

I noticed that Tina seemed very sleepy. I worried that she was not doing well with this pregnancy and perhaps was anemic. "Have you seen the *comadroña* [trained midwife]?"

"We can't afford a comadroña. She usually charges ten quetzales for a delivery, so I will wait until the time is due and then call a *partera* [lay midwife] who charges only two quetzales. I wish I weren't pregnant. I would like not to have my babies so close together; they are so weak, and two have already died. How can you want more when you hear them cry all day and night because they are hungry? Jorge doesn't hear them. He's out in the field."

Tina continued, "I am afraid to use some of the herbs others use to cause the pregnancy to end; I don't know what to do." Tina described herbal teas, made from dried, local plant leaves used by some women in the town to cause abortions. Her stories were a mix of old wives' tales and actual ethnobotany. "Some women die when they take these; some hemorrhage," she concluded.

"Yes, I know about some of them, but I think it is wiser to take something to protect you from getting pregnant. Don't they have contraceptive pills and injections at the *salud de pública* [health clinic] that you could take?"

"Yes, but I'm afraid to use the pill, because I hear that it causes cancer, and that it has all sorts of evil powers. My friend took some, and her baby died when she was nursing him. Besides, we need our sons to work in the fields and when the girls are older, they will work in the City," she concluded.

"I think you should talk this over with that nice female doctor who gave you the Incaparina today; she might have some advice for you." At times like this, it was a dilemma for me not to give nursing care advice. As an anthropologist, I was open to learning the emic views of events and issues, but as a nurse, I had knowledge that could help my informants. Whenever I was asked a health question, I tried to frame my answers within the context of the question only. I volunteered medical information only when I knew it would help an informant avoid a dangerous situation. My first alliance was to my informants, to protect them only if I felt I had information that would fit within their cultural worlds.

Although the Hernández family did not attend church, they considered themselves Catholic. "I think you should have as many babies as God wants you to have," Tina answered sadly.

As I thought about her remark, I looked into her face, which was quite beautiful, even without her teeth. Tina had very large, soft-brown eyes, and high cheekbones. Her frail body seemed to be strong, as she had already carried several buckets of water from the stream. "I think we'll go down to the river to wash the clothes," Tina decided. "The stream water is too muddy; it will be better below. There are also rocks down there to pound the clothes on."

As long as I had lived in Zaragoza, I had never been down to the "river," but I had heard about it often. Tina prepared Baby Miguel in a shirt and wrapped him in a blanket. The two daughters, Juanita and Dahlia, ages five and four, had been playing with some sticks in the mud; they walked quickly ahead of us, carrying small baskets of clothes in their hands. I carried a basket too. The river was located about two kilometers down a winding path and through several cornfields. The scenery at the bottom of the hill was beautiful.

Bushes lined the river, which was very shallow and only about ten feet in width, but the water seemed clear and clean.

"Jorge will bring water for our cooking later this evening," Tina smiled. I thought about how comfortably I lived, with my water faucet in the kitchen that poured forth abundant water with a touch of my hand. How hard it is for the poorest people to get even the basic necessities of life.

Tina and I laid the dirty shirts and trousers on some rocks and then scrubbed them with a harsh, black soap Tina had bought at the local market. Using a plastic bucket, we poured river water over them again and again. We spread the cleaned clothes on the grass surrounding the river. I didn't see her wash many things that she or the daughters wore and wondered why. Perhaps they didn't have changes of clothes? Their clothes were indeed quite grimy. When we finished the washing, we sat quietly by the side of the river and ate the beans and tortillas that Tina had carried down to the river wrapped in a cloth.

"Do you need some kindling for the fire?" I asked, hoping to be helpful.

"The boys can get some when they come back from the fields. I have enough for today," was Tina's reply. I had discovered another cultural difference. In Patzún the women carried most of the firewood for the family's needs.

After a couple of hours, the clothes were almost dry, so we picked them up and started up the hill again. Tina and her daughters with their bare feet could walk much better than I with my shoes on— my loafers kept slipping on the damp earth. When we finally reached the top, I was exhausted. Baby Miguel seldom cried or made noises; he didn't seem very alert for a six-month-old. I hoped he wasn't sick.

Tina suggested that we have a siesta; I was very pleased, since I was very tired and perhaps a little bored. There wasn't much to talk about; I wondered if Tina felt like this much of the day. We each stretched out on a grass mat; there was little life around the cane hut except for the chickens that walked around outside. I looked at the inside of the house; it seemed temporary, impermanent. The walls were grass mats tied together around poles of various sizes. There were a few shelves of wood for holding cooking and eating utensils, a small mirror, and several nails, on which were hung a couple of pants and shirts. There were no calendars or pictures and no sacred corn such as I had seen in the house of the brujo in Xajáxac. I didn't see any books or toys. It looked and felt dismal. Poor.

At about five o'clock, Jorge, Juan, and Franco returned from the fields; they looked very tired, and their toes and hands were filled with mud. Tina asked them to get some water for cooking, so they each took a plastic bucket and began the two-kilometer walk to the river below. About an hour later they reappeared, looking quite clean, so I assumed they had bathed in the water as well. We ate supper—beans, rice, and tortillas—by the light of a candle. Each "place setting" consisted of a big soup dish and a large tablespoon.

After brushing my teeth, I lay down in my sleeping bag, exhausted, not so much from being overstimulated, but rather from the sadness of the conditions. I wanted to avoid thinking about the lives of the Hernández family and others in the same economic state. The Hernández family had few resources, and they seemed to suffer from malaise—from sadness or perhaps from being anemic or ill (maybe all three). Tina and Jorge had no friends and hadn't seen their families for many years. They weren't connected with the church or with the school system. How lonely and helpless their lives seemed. Was this the culture that Oscar Lewis (1962) proclaimed kept poor people poor? Without resources and a social network to facilitate moving out of poverty, would Tina and Jorge perpetuate this lifeway in their children? Where would dreams and hopes originate if not in the family? I slept fretfully that night, and awakened when Jorge and his sons arose at four o'clock in the morning to go back into the fields. I got up after they left and told Tina that I would go home, too, and perhaps she could sleep a bit longer. She did. As I walked down the street to my house, I had mixed feelings about living with this family of the lowest income level. I could change and go about my life, because I had choices, but what choices did they have except to survive, day by day?

Back in my home, I wrote my fieldnotes about the Hernández family; the memory of these struggling individuals was etched forever in my mind. It's never easy. Sometimes fieldworkers carry burdens in their minds and hearts that never show up in their fieldnotes. In 1975 I carried a burden for the Hernández family. It seemed that for them life's only hope was to survive, a little at a time. Perhaps things could change . . .

Chapter 11

Surviving as a Corporate, Cooperative Unit
The Indian Family

What hurts Indians most is that our costumes are considered
beautiful, but it's as if the person wearing it didn't exist.
—Rigoberta Menchú, *I, Rigoberta Menchú: An Indian Woman
in Guatemala*, 1992

Family life differs in the two towns I studied. Some of the differences
are related to their very different households. Most of the families
in Patzún live in compound housing structures. By living within
this type of family system, I learned about economic interdepend-
ence based on a strong kinship network and a patrilineal inheritance
system. I also learned more about Indian women and their worldview, dreams, and aspirations.

Cooperation Makes a Productive Home

The Maczul family had held land for seven generations near
Patzún, and because the patzuñeros retain a patrilineal inheritance
system they had kept the land combined rather than splitting it
further and further into smaller plots. Such an inheritance places
blood relatives, consanguineous kin, into closer alliance than it does
the affinal relatives, or those related by marriage. In Patzún, this
patrilineal kinship system is basic to all negotiations done within

and outside the household. In such a system, women are dependent upon the male, because they don't directly receive an inheritance. On the other hand, women, especially mothers, do have decision-making power, which comes from being in a respectable position (that of mother of sons, and of course, wives who could produce sons). Although sons are preferred, women in Patzún spoke of needing daughters, both to help with the work and to enjoy. Mother Maczul had once declared, "My daughters are *mi luz de la vida* [light of my life]." Mothers and daughters spend a lot of time together, walking, working, and seemingly enjoying one another with laughter.

When a daughter marries, she moves into the house of her husband's family. New brides are considered a mixed blessing in Patzún: they provide household support, but they also add to already-overcrowded compound houses. This tradition seems to cause more problems than solutions, yet the people of Patzún don't want to move to less populated areas. Maria Maczul frequently commented, "I never want to move away from Patzún, as I would miss my mother too much." When asked, "Who is your ideal female?" almost 100 percent of the patzuñeras reply, "My mother, because she is kind and helps people." The ideal characterological traits among the people of Patzún are getting along with people and being kind. There is no expression of self-sacrifice among patzuñeras as is common among the zaragozañas.

Women are highly visible in the society of Patzún. They negotiate in the market and help with the corn harvest. They laugh and gossip in the streets, in the markets, and at the pila as they daily wash their clothes. Their contribution to the household economy is significant and also, I believe, a source of their power. This cultural pattern of participation is in part necessitated by the structure of a compound household. Of course, not everyone is kind and cooperative, though this has become a stereotype of Indian people.

On a Sunday Afternoon

One day I witnessed a confrontation which assured me that not all Indians are tranquil and cooperative. It was a sunny Sunday, the major market day in Patzún. I had already gone to mass, returned to the Maczuls' compound, and eaten at the neighbor's comedor. After resting and reading a bit, I decided to walk to the market to buy some local herbs. It was toward the end of the market day, and people were beginning to pack up their goods and go home. As I walked along the street I noticed several men walking in groups

Washing clothes at Patzún pila, laughing and gossiping

and laughing, and who had apparently been drinking. Drinking and getting drunk on Sunday is a well-known pastime in Patzún and other Indian towns. Friends had warned me to be cautious when driving on Sundays, because the men, especially, are inebriated by the late afternoon. Many accidents occur on the winding mountain highways as drunken men fall into, or crawl onto, the roads. A driver might come around a corner and screech to an immediate halt, because a drunken man had sprawled in the middle of the highway. (I never saw an inebriated woman, although women were known to get drunk at times.) I was always alert when driving on Sunday afternoons.

Among the men walking toward me, I noticed one in particular who was very drunk and staggering down the road. He swayed from side to side, his eyes half-closed. Several men along the way noticed his vulnerability, and as he stumbled and staggered, laughter began to rise from the gathering crowd. He fell once, then picked himself up, and fell yet again; then he crawled like a bug for a while and soon tried standing again. The crowd grew larger and more derisive, chanting at and chiding the drunken man. Laughter swelled from the mob, and I heard several people call, "Animal!"

Next, a clod of dirt came flying past me and hit the man, square on his forehead. He looked shocked and frightened. Then more clods of dirt flew by, some hitting his body, and more hitting his face. The clods turned into rocks, as more of the crowd joined the heavy rain of torment. Finally, the entire crowd—close to fifty people—had joined in, and the laughter became a roar. What was I, a witness to the slaughter, to do? The man began to bleed heavily around his eyes and mouth. My heart pounded harder and harder, and I terribly wanted the pelting to stop. He was lying on the ground, curled up to protect his face and body. I resisted crying and running away.

At the point when the man appeared to be losing consciousness, a loud shout came from the side of the road. An older woman, all alone, came forward, turning from side to side; she, alone, berated the crowd, telling them what she thought in a loud Cakchiquel voice. The crowd backed off, stunned by her forceful accusations, grew quiet, and slowly slunk away. Silence. The drunken man lay bleeding and still. Suppose he's dead, I thought. Then a younger woman, perhaps his wife, came with a wheelbarrow. She and the older woman lifted the weakened, unconscious man into the wheelbarrow and carried him away. I struggled to assimilate what I had just witnessed. Just then the cathedral bells pealed the announcement of another mass. I planned to attend—again. I had to break the spell of what I had just witnessed.

Inside the massive cathedral were about 400 Indians, women and men intermingled. The thick thud of their bare feet was a type of musical rhythm, as they rose, then knelt during the service. The thick callouses on their feet showed like large tumors in their kneeling positions. The smell was unforgettable, their smoke-filled traje pungent in contrast to the sweet-smelling incense.

The altar was far more ornate than the simple blue and white one in Zaragoza. The cathedral was ablaze with gold and silver, a witness of the wealth that had been donated for it. On the altar cloth was a phrase from the Bible written in Cakchiquel: "Bread of Life." Padre Sergio, the priest from Colégio San Bernardino, said the mass—half in Spanish, half in Cakchiquel—assisted by Indian altar boys. The vision of the pelting rocks faded as I heard the call to "love one another." I felt restored, if still somewhat unsettled.

Thumbprints on Newsprint

My old friend, Edith, the British midwife who worked with the Behrhorst Program, had developed and managed an "under-five clinic" every Wednesday in Patzún, to assess the health of children five years old and under and to educate mothers about proper feeding and child rearing. The clinic was held in the courtyard of one of the Indian mothers, Hortensia, who was president of the Women's Club (my etic term for the social group of women in Patzún) and a mother of three children (two daughters and a son, all under the age of five). Her family was wealthier than most in the town; their compound home was large, with a spacious courtyard that was often filled with bundles of corn from the harvests. Hortensia was friendly, smiling, and open to new ideas. During the harvest season she worked hard in the fields, beside her husband, Ernesto. Her home was spotless, her dress impeccable. Hortensia was a role model for the women in Patzún, so it was natural that the Women's Club meetings were held in her home each Wednesday. The club was organized by women interested in learning together about such topics as health care and ways of improving their own education. The club had two goals: health care for the women's children and literacy for themselves, an accomplishment they could pass on after it was achieved. The Indian woman's strong desire to become literate in Spanish is so powerfully spoken by Rigoberta Menchú (1992), "They've always said, poor Indians they can't speak, so many speak for them. That's why I decided to learn Spanish" (157).

My role, as an anthropologist, was to assist Hortensia, the hostess, in setting up the scales and measuring tapes. On Wednesdays the storage shed in the courtyard was converted into a measuring and weighing room. Each mother brought her children under the age of five—some had as many as three—into the storage shed. Inside, the shed was clean and dry. The scales were simple; there was little expense in the equipment. The only expense to the mother was fifteen centavos for a month's supply of vitamins, if the mother chose to buy them. No medications were given at this under-five clinic; the goal was to teach mothers how to improve the daily care of their children by giving them nutritious food. Immunizations for childhood diseases such as diphtheria, measles, smallpox, whooping cough, and polio were given at the salud de pública.

Outside the weighing and measuring shed were two chairs and a table, where Edith would talk privately to each mother about her children's health. Edith would then listen with a stethoscope to the heart sounds of each child, and she would also examine the mouth, throat, and ears of each one. The children's height and weight were recorded on a card kept by the mother. If Edith found a child was not growing at an expected rate, she would advise the mother about seeking medical care. The clinic was a means of screening children for potentially serious problems, such as malnutrition, intestinal worms, or infection. The mothers and children considered Edith a

Hortensia, president of Patzún Women's Club, and her three children in compound where literacy classes were held (in the background are piles of harvested corn)

friend; she would talk with everyone, and they would laugh with her.

The under-five clinic lasted for about an hour, after which the mothers would form a circle on the earthen floor inside Hortensia's house. The children would play outside, safe in the courtyard. Rather than sitting and gossiping, the women were all learning to read. Yes, what an exciting experience! In Patzún 95 percent of women over the age of twenty were illiterate. Younger girls and children were attending local schools and learning to read and write, but older women had been kept away from such opportunities; Hortensia was one of those women. The members of the Women's Club were determined to be able to read and write, as was evident by their faithful attendance. Week after week, they arrived carrying their well-worn reading booklets.

These patzuñeras were also eager to learn about the health of their children. In Patzún, women, in particular, were interested in nutrition. The wife of President Carlos Araña Orsorio, who was president during my 1974 study year, had created an awareness of nutrition and had also promoted various feeding programs in the rural areas. It was clear that for the women of Patzún becoming literate was tied with improving the lives of their children. They also expressed a desire to become more independent in and knowledgeable about business negotiations that were conducted in Spanish and which often included written agreements. The patzuñeras knew that being able to read and write Spanish would give them an advantage in dealing with Ladinos and tourists.

In Zaragoza there were no women's clubs or nutritional clinics. The Guatemalan nuns who lived across the street from me in Zaragoza told me several times that they had tried to organize a women's club, but that the effort had always failed. There weren't any cooperatives in Zaragoza; in contrast, there were three cooperatives just for women in Patzún. These cooperatives would purchase bulk quantities of materials in Guatemala City for embroidering. They also organized savings and loan programs, acting much like a bank. There were also six cooperatives for men in Patzún, which aided them in marketing corn; there were none in Zaragoza. The cultural norms in the towns are obvious. The Indians are a cooperative economic unit, and the Ladinos are competitive and individualistic. None of these terms are value terms; they merely describe the cultural norms of the two towns as I observed them.

Edith and I used comic books in teaching the patzuñeras to read. The simple language plus the appealing pictures made concepts easier to grasp. Writing was a little harder for the patzuñeras to learn, but each week we could see progress. Women were starting to sign their names. The openness they showed in confronting their illiteracy was exciting. They would laugh about mistakes and tease one another. In this interaction was a strong support, unlike anything available to the women living alone in Zaragoza.

Hortensia would greet us at the gate each Wednesday morning around nine. Her round, rosy cheeks and wide-open smile were a welcoming sight. One day, however, our arrival was met by six Jeeps parked outside the compound.

Edith cried, "Oh, oh! There's trouble!"

As we opened the big gate into the compound, Hortensia was not there. Instead, soldiers armed with machine guns lined the compound wall. There were about twenty men, and the leader, a giant man about six and a half feet tall, stood aiming a machine gun right at Edith.

Edith, in her nonchalant manner, said a customary greeting: "Good morning. How are you today?"

The leader, a stern-looking man, stepped forward and said, "We have come to arrest you for practicing medicine without a license."

Hortensia and the other women were now pressing against the wall, having come out of the house, but they were huddled away from the soldiers, looking very frightened. The children peeked out from behind their mothers' skirts, which they were hugging tightly, obviously frightened as well.

"That's silly," replied the brave midwife. "What do you mean, 'practicing medicine'? I'm a midwife, and I'm here only to weigh and measure the children and to teach the mothers how to prevent malnutrition. You know the president's wife has nutritional programs all over the Republic. Why do you think I am practicing medicine?"

The tall man, the chief public health officer of the Department of Chimaltenango, replied sternly, "Let me see what you do and how you do it!"

As on all other Wednesdays, Edith and I went about our work, setting up the scales, the measuring tapes, and the table and chairs. We placed the vitamins on the table.

The chief said, triumphantly, "I see that you do have bottles of pills."

"Those are only vitamins," Edith explained emphatically. We went about our business.

"And who are you?" the public health officer asked, pointing to me.

"I'm an anthropologist from the United States," I answered with a tremble in my voice, "and I help to weigh and measure the children in the shed."

"Hmph!" he snorted.

Several children and their mothers timidly went through the usual routine of talking with Edith and getting weighed and measured.

After about fifteen minutes, the chief officer came forward and said, "We are closing you down, because you do not have proper sanitary conditions here."

Edith chuckled, "You know that the water in the fountain is from the city and that the seat of the latrine has a stamp on it that reads 'Inspected by the Public Health Department.' If these aren't sanitary, then what is?"

The officer looked frustrated. Finally he said, "Well, you don't have proper lighting in the shed for weighing and measuring the children. Come in and I'll show you." We followed him into the shed. The officer closed the shutters and slammed the door shut. Edith, the tall officer, and I stood in pitch darkness for several minutes. I had to stifle a giggle, as we three stood shoulder to shoulder in the darkness.

"I guess you're right," replied Edith with resignation. I didn't say a word.

With triumph, the tall health officer and the twenty machine-gunned soldiers silently left the compound. Edith explained to the women that we could not meet anymore until this matter was cleared by the officials. "I hope that you continue to learn to read and write on your own and together. We'll return as soon as the matter is cleared up."

Several women had tears in their eyes, but none spoke.

"We must leave right away," said Edith, "because the soldiers will soon return to see if we have gone, as they have ordered us to. I don't want to be arrested. I'd suggest that everyone just go home—quietly."

Edith and I returned to Chimaltenango and told the story to Doc Behrhorst. "I'm disappointed," said Doc, "but I guess we could have predicted that he would try to corner us somehow, so he used the Women's Club to do it. What a coward. We'll stay quiet for awhile and see what the Indians themselves do."

Several weeks later, Edith came to my house and exclaimed, "Look what Hortensia and the women did!" She pulled out of her car a huge roll of white newsprint paper and began to unroll it on my living-room floor. Thumbprint after thumbprint marched down the side of the paper with now and then a "beginning" signature. One hundred, 300, 500, no, 800!! Eight hundred thumbprints marked the women's protest to the cancellation of literacy classes. Eight hundred illiterate women had expressed their power—their right to learn to read and write. They protested with their thumbprints the closing of the under-five clinic and their literacy classes, for they knew the power that learning could bring to them and their families, and their children yet to come. Others, too—such as the public health officer—knew that literacy would empower the women and thus, cowardly, chose to keep the women powerless, at least for long as possible. When I left Guatemala in 1975, the under-five clinic was still prohibited from reopening, and no one was helping the women to overcome their illiteracy.

Chapter 12

Cane Huts, Rats, and Snakes

Our best hope is that we can come to care positively about the diversity of human beings and ally ourselves with many different groups, all of whom we think of as "we."
—Margaret Mead, *Some Personal Views*, 1979

Many of the women in Patzún were trying to overcome their poverty—by becoming literate and by seeking health care for their children. But were there others who were lost in their own problems, as I had found in the Hernández family in Zaragoza? I only knew that I needed to find out how the poorest-of-the-poor lived in Patzún.

Seeking a Connection

It was hardly daylight, just the soft gray of early morning. It had been a dream-filled night. As I lay in my warm sleeping bag on a pile of pine needles in the middle of the cane hut, I reminisced about how I had come to spend the night with the Caj family in Patzún. Remembering the previous day, I first thought about how I needed to learn more about—to connect more with—the lives of the poorest-of-the-poor in Patzún. Then I recalled seeing the hut of the Caj family in the small valley, surrounded by bushes and set aside from other huts in the town. It looked as if it were about to fall down; I had thought that many times as I passed by on the way to the cathedral and the plaza. Who lives there? I wondered. The thatched roof hung close to the ground, and it looked lopsided, as if someone could just give it a push and over it would tumble.

"Maria, do you know who lives in that cane hut in the middle of the valley?" I described it to my assistant interviewer one day.

"Yes, but not very well. They are poor folks."

"Would you mind going with me to ask them if I could stay in their home for a night and part of the day?" I knew that since they were poor, they probably spoke only Cakchiquel, so I needed Maria as an interpreter.

Maria had grown accustomed to my strange requests and didn't ask me why. "Yes, of course, I'll go with you, but what shall I tell them?"

"Tell them that I am a woman from the United States who is living with the Maczul family and who is writing a story about Patzún. And that by staying overnight with them, I'd be better able to describe how the people live. Also tell them that I will pay fifteen quetzales for the rent and for food. Would that be enough?"

"Of course that would be enough!" Maria laughed, knowing that the annual income was about 150 quetzales for the poorest families. With that we walked together down the path that led to the courtyard of the cane hut. A woman dressed in the usual red and blue huipil and blue wraparound skirt was grinding corn on a mano and matete—her baby was held on her back in a rebozo. As we approached her, she looked up and rose to her feet. I noticed that she seemed relaxed, was small in stature, and was toothless. She appeared to be about thirty-five years old. There were no other people in the courtyard.

Maria began talking with her in Cakchiquel; the woman looked at me, quite openly, smiled, and nodded her head. They continued talking for a bit, and then Maria turned to me and said, "Her name is Concepción Caj; her husband's name is Leonardo, and they have three children: Lucío, age eight; Felicía, age six; and the baby, Hermando, age two. She speaks some Spanish, so she can talk with you; her husband also speaks some Spanish. He apparently is an alcoholic and doesn't work. The only income they have is from her sales of weavings, and also sometimes Leonardo works in the fields during harvest."

"Please tell her many thanks and that I would like to come tomorrow and spend the day with her, doing what she does. Also tell her that I will bring water with a special container, so she doesn't worry about getting me water [which was always a problem in the dry season]. I also will bring my sleeping bag, so she doesn't need to use her ponchos." I tried always to be careful to impose as little as possible on the limited resources of the Indians, as there was little food or water in most of the lower-income homes.

Maria looked pleased, so I assumed I had explained things pretty well. They talked a bit more. Maria added, "She will look for you around eight in the morning. She needs to get some firewood tomorrow and wonders if you could drive your car to a place where there is some wood around."

"That's a good idea," I answered, knowing well what a problem it was to get enough firewood for cooking, and I thought I could show my understanding through the small gesture. "I'd also like to give her two quetzales to get some tortillas for our trip tomorrow." I knew Concepción probably wouldn't have time to grind the masa for the tortillas before we left in the morning.

"I told her that you were kind and easy to get along with, but she can see that now," laughed Maria.

I came to Concepción's house at eight o'clock as planned. I drove my car down the gully rather than leaving it on the hilltop. Concepción was washing clothes in a small bucket with Baby Hermando on her back. She smiled when she saw me and asked if I would like some coffee. Since I could see that she had placed a pot of water over the open fire, I said, "Yes, thank you," wanting to be polite. She leaned over the hot coals, picked up the pot, poured hot water into an enameled tin cup, and pointed with a spoon to the instant coffee jar. I fixed my own cup of coffee, noticing that she wasn't going to have any. Just then the children, Lucío and Felicía, came out of the hut. Their only toys seemed to be some sticks and a small ball. Their clothes were patched but clean. Having finished washing the shirts and pants, Concepción laid them on a patch of green grass near the cane fence, where they would quickly dry in the sun. Concepción placed eight tortillas in a small towel and filled a bottle with water from a jug in the hut. We were now ready for the trip to get firewood.

The children sat in the back seat, the baby, Concepción, and I in the front. They all chattered in Cakchiquel and were obviously excited to be riding in a car. I knew where we were going, as I had walked in that area with other friends. The view was spectacular, with barrancas almost a mile deep and heavily lined with trees— an excellent spot in which to gather firewood. We turned onto a rutted dirt road, my Opel Kadette bouncing over the rough terrain. Suddenly the road dropped out of sight. I immediately stopped the car and got out to inspect the area. The road dropped a sheer four feet—apparently the heavy rains several months earlier had caused the road to cave in. I stepped around the car to Concepción's window and told her that it was impossible to drive further. She kept saying, "Go on, go on, the wood is ahead." I tried to make her understand that the car couldn't drive down that sheer cliff. Finally she understood, and everybody got out of the car and began walking

Back-breaking scrubbing with an infant on one's back

down the road, laughing. It was a great adventure.

We walked about a mile without picking up any firewood. The fields were just being planted with corn, and Concepción warned, "Women must not cross the fields during this time, because the grain will spoil and die." I understood her concern, having heard the myth about a menstruating woman's power to destroy planted seed. Finally, we reached a spot in the road that was pleasant and shady. We stopped and Concepción unwrapped the cold tortillas; we each had two and drank our water. That was lunch. Then we started back to the car picking up dry kindling and wood along the way. The children gathered small sticks—their eyes could spy just the right size for making a fire, whereas mine seemed blind to all but the worst wood. Concepción had made a *nido* (nest) by wrapping a towel in a circle and placed it on her head. Then she placed a basket on top of the nido and began filling the basket with firewood.

The stack of wood—gathered so tediously—grew taller and taller, until it was at least two feet high. Concepción would bend down, pick up wood, put it into the basket, then put it on her head and continue walking—with her two-year-old baby wrapped snugly in the rebozo on her back. It was an amazing feat of strength and balance.

When we finally reached the car, the basket was towering with wood; both children were also carrying large bundles of their own. Mine was the smallest bundle, barely a half foot in diameter. I tried to lift Concepción's basket after she had placed it on the ground but could barely raise it more than a foot, let alone place it on my head and walk with a baby on my back. I reflected on that experience as I lay in bed the next morning. I thought about how Concepción couldn't understand the limitations of my car near the cliff, and how I, in turn, couldn't understand her strength, after having eaten only two tortillas. Somehow our individual understandings meet the needs of surviving in our own respective cultures. Our worlds are so different, yet in both, parents have the responsibility to teach and train their children to perform the tasks necessary for survival.

With the trunk of my car bursting with firewood, we headed back to Patzún and to the rest of the day. The children continued to play and occasionally interrupted their games to fetch something for Concepción. The baby slept most of the afternoon. Concepción invited me into the hut to show me her home. It reminded me of the home of the brujo in Xajáxac. In one area were a few tall jugs for water and one for masa to make tortillas. I saw ponchos in one corner, but no other furniture. The mano and metate were leaning against the wall, so I knew that Concepción could not afford to have her corn ground by the molinera. The cane walls were held in place with various poles, and mud filled in the cracks. The thick thatched roof was held in place by one large pole in the middle of the room. The earthen floor had worn smooth from use and looked cleanly swept. The space was much smaller than it appeared from the outside, but was warm and cozy.

Handicapped Handiwork to Make a Living

Concepción gathered some unbleached cotton cloth stamped with designs of the symbols of the Catholic church. She took some thread from a basket, and we went back outside into the bright sunlight so that she might begin her handiwork. She was embroidering cloths to be used in religious processions; however, most were not given to the church but instead were bought by tourists who came through the town on their way to Lake Atitlán. I remembered my mother, in Colorado, had made embroidered dish towels and pillow cases using a similar process. She would buy "transfer patterns" at the local dime store. She would place each pattern over its chosen spot on the towel or pillow case. Next, Mother would carefully iron the transfer tissue. The cotton cloth would then be ready for Mother to stich with colorful embroidery threads. She had made beautiful designs of flowers, birds, and baskets.

Concepción embroidered in bright blues, reds, and yellows, usually creating symbols of the Catholic church, such as a dove representing the Holy Spirit, a chalice and wafer indicating the communion cup, and a lamb symbolizing Jesus. Her stitches were very uneven and loose, not the patterned, taut stitches I had become accustomed to seeing in the market. I wondered to whom she actually sold her weavings and embroidery work, because, by most standards, they were not well crafted. As I watched her more closely, I realized that her eyesight was probably poor. I asked her if she could read.

"No, I never went to school," she answered. "I began to live with Leonardo when I was sixteen and he was seventeen. Our parents had died, and we needed each other. We lived with my aunt in one of the hamlets outside of town. My grandfather owned *this* house, and when he died, my aunt gave it to us. It's about fifty years old and not in good repair, but it is our home.

"I had miscarriages right away, then we had two children and later the baby. I'm twenty-eight years old [she looked much older], and Leonardo is twenty-nine. He began to drink soon after we were married, and now he is drunk most of the time. Everyone calls him the town drunk. I'm very sad, because he is a good man, but he can't stay away from the bottle. I never give him any money. I wish Lucío and Felicia could go to school, but when I took them to the Catholic parochial school, the nuns didn't seem to like them, so the children didn't want to go back. [Note: This parochial school was *not* the Colégio San Bernardino.] Then the evangelicals came to our house for several years and wanted us to join their church, but it was hard for me to make the change from the Catholic church. Now they don't come by anymore. I don't have any friends—because of Leonardo, I think. My aunt is my only hope; she gives me money from the harvest, but just a little. Soon Lucío can earn money in the harvest. I'm sure he can help with carrying the corn—you saw how strong he is. Felicia helps my aunt, and that gives us some money for corn to eat. I wish I could sell more of my weavings—I work on them almost everyday." (I did buy one large piece and have it in my office, reminding me often of Concepción's plight.)

The shadows were growing longer when Leonardo came walking down the path. He had spent the day in the plaza, talking to friends and perhaps drinking. Leonardo had a slight build and a handsome, smiling face, though he looked much older than twenty-nine years. He greeted the children and Concepción with laughter and playful hugging. They seemed happy to see him. Concepción introduced me to him; he bowed his head slightly in a greeting and smiled. Leonardo seemed quite comfortable with my presence. He took Baby Hermando and played with him on his lap while Concepción began preparing the black beans, rice, and tortillas for supper. I was very, very hungry, as two tortillas for lunch was less than I usually ate. We sat around the small fire, enclosed by the customary cinder blocks and a grill, and ate our supper from white enameled soup dishes using large spoons. It was simple but very tasty.

Birth Control?

Concepción had shown me the latrine early in the day, so when it seemed it was time to retire, I carried my jar of water to the latrine and brushed my teeth and washed my face. The children were in their ponchos when I came back, and Concepción and Leonardo were talking. I asked them about their family, being concerned that they seemed to have so few options for improvement or change. They said they were happy: "We have our children; the house is ours, and so far our health is good. We don't have many friends, but we have our aunt and some cousins; we're better off than some people.

"But we do want our children to go to school and to be better off than we are. Sometimes I want to go to mass, but I am ashamed of my clothes and that I don't read and write. I wish I had running water; sometimes I have to go to the pila at three in the morning in order to have water. No one saves me a place in line during the day." Concepción continued sadly, "I don't want my daughter to do only weaving; I want her to be a teacher or a nurse."

I thought about these simple needs, and the more complex desires, as I crawled into my sleeping bag, wondering if I could sleep.

It was in that gray light of dawn that I lay preparing to get up. I heard Concepción cough, and then the children. Leonardo snored softly. As my eyes became more accustomed to the grayness, I thought I saw something resting above my left foot. It seemed to be dangling in midair, and it wasn't more than two feet from my foot. I tried to avoid recognizing it, but, yes, I realized that it wasn't a shadow but a large, five-foot, black snake—at least three inches in diameter. I was petrified. Could it be poisonous? I sucked in air from fright. Concepción must have heard me, because she awakened. She looked over at me, grinned, and began to laugh. "Oh, you see our *apresador rata* [rat catcher]," she exclaimed. "We need to have snakes to keep the rats away from our corn and the children."

I shuddered, thinking about which would be the easier to live with on a daily basis—rats or snakes—and figured Concepción was right. Rats are more of a problem than a helpful snake. Rats carry germs for typhus and other diseases, and they do eat corn and sometimes bite children. A greater respect for the basics of the food cycle seemed to creep into my thinking upon living so close to other creatures.

Concepción rubbed her eyes and started to lift her legs out from her poncho. As she did so, the long, slithering snake (Slinky, as I called him) went up the pole to the thatched roof, not to be seen again until perhaps that night. We, too, knew the day had begun, so after a walk down the path to the latrine, Concepción and I came back to start the fire and the day.

Leonardo left for the plaza soon after breakfast, the children played with their sticks and ball, and Concepción began weaving with a back-strap loom a cloth the colors of Patzún—bright red and blue. She talked about family again, and this time I asked her if she wanted more children. "Oh, no, but the choice is not ours," she said. "It's up to God; he knows how many I should have."

"So you don't use any type of protection?" I asked.

"No," she replied. "You know Leonardo's drinking makes it so he can't do it." I assumed that his impotence was her protection, that perhaps he was unable to have sex anymore.

"How are you able to feed your family?" I asked. "I've seen how difficult life is for you."

"I make about two quetzales a week selling the weavings, and my daughter works for my aunt and earns about five quetzales a month. Lucío earns about five quetzales a week during harvest. When we add it all together, we make about 150 quetzales a year [about the same amount the Hernández family of Zaragoza earned]. I need my children to help us. They don't ask for much. We each have one change of clothing, and Leonardo has three shirts, but they are very old. I think our house is going to fall down; then maybe I will move in with my aunt."

I had learned of the rhythm and some of the meaning of life from this family, one of the poorest in Patzún—I'd made connections. As I prepared to leave I thought about how the Caj family held itself

Cane hut—for people, snakes, and rats

together—with some affection and family ties but with little or no social support from the outside, not even from the church and schools. They survived by relying on their own wits and their small family connections.

I concluded that the women of Patzún are more assertive and organized than the women of Zaragoza; however, each group has had to adapt ways of living to separate cultural systems of sanctions and rewards. One system is not better than the other, but they are different. The poorest-of-the-poor are similar in each town, but still distinct. Both rely almost solely on their nuclear family resources, whether the male or the female is the income producer. Outside circumstances or unexpected events and their state of health are the reasons for their poor fortune.

Chapter 13

Get an Ark
Hurricane Fifi Hits

Agua . . . this ancient volcano fills with water and has burst in
the past to enter unpredictably into modern history. Its brush
by the sun, however, is as predictable as anything on earth.
—Carroll Behrhorst, in *A New Dawn in Guatemala*,
Richard Luecke, ed., 1993

Finding rhyme and reason for everything seems to be a human
condition. We humans seem to search for reasons when sometimes,
like the poorest-of-the-poor families in both Zaragosa and Patzún,
we just have to accept circumstances and events. The next two
chapters deal with unpredictable circumstances and events that
arose in the two towns in 1974 and explain what the townspeople
did to cope with them.

No Signs of Trouble . . . I Thought

The sky had a lime green look to it that day. The transistor radio
had warned of a coming hurricane, but no one in Zaragoza seemed
concerned, because the announcer had said that Fifi was in the Gulf
of Mexico, at least 500 miles south—or so I thought. The rainy
season had been the usual monsoonal type—clear morning skies,
followed by the heavens simply opening up at about four in the
afternoon. Steady rain would continue afterward, with lots of
lightning and thunder throughout the night. The rain was

welcomed, as the dry season had sucked up the very breath of the fields, leaving the ground dusty and unnourished. During the dry season, every living thing had turned brown; tempers had flared, and the scorching equatorial sun had seemed to penetrate to the bone. The rain was necessary to sustain the resultant meager crops of maize so that all would not go hungry. Hungry children means low resistance to infection. The depleted antibodies of infants aren't enough to resist infection and sustain life, as I had learned in Chimaltenango in 1971 when Baby Rosa died in her mother's arms.

Was danger near? I had learned to watch my neighbors for clues. They knew the signs that I seemed to miss. I took my cues about danger from them. Just as I had relied on the signals from my mother as to who was a good man or who was a bad man for me to dance with at the Corpus Christi Fiesta, so I relied on the judgment of the zaragozaños and patzuñeros for most of my actions. But on this morning, it was time for me to drive into Antigua for some typing supplies and to check on the latest news about the impeachment of President Nixon (far away, Watergate compelled Western attention) and other world events. I suspected no problem from Hurricane Fifi.

Pablo, Silvia, and their two daughters had gone to see Silvia's family in Quétzaltenango, a beautiful Indian town four hours away, and weren't returning for another week. They had simply locked the doors to the two tiendas and got on a bus. "We do this once a year," Silvia had said matter-of-factly. I missed seeing them several times a day, but since I was very busy with the household survey, I had not really noticed that no one was around to do the usual hitchhiking (Silvia or Pablo usually were the ones to tell others of my upcoming trips). Perhaps I should have been suspicious. Sometimes I would announce my intention to make a trip into Antigua or Chimaltenango the day before and then have to brace myself against the number of people who would try to fit into my tiny car. The largest number had been thirteen people, which left me with almost no room to steer the car or to reach the brakes. This time I took off up the highway, alone and quietly relieved to have an hour or so to myself, as my days and evenings were usually filled with visitors or my own talking with neighbors around town. I was almost never alone.

The roads to Antigua were dry and clear; I pressed onward over the winding hills and steep valleys. The corn stood tall and heavy with full-kerneled ears. Soon we'd have the harvest and all the celebrations that go with it. I felt so fortunate to be able to share in this experience. I had outlived my culture shock and now was heavily involved in the cultural systems of each town. It was the middle of August and I, too, truly felt the joy of the upcoming harvest; this was my home now, and these were my friends, with whom I would rejoice.

Culture Shock in the Form of Lemon Pie

Driving peacefully along, I reminisced about one of those incidents when my culture shock was most evident. This incident had occurred during my fourth month of fieldwork. I was living in the Maczuls' compound house in Patzún. There were four families living there. The families included Mother and Father Maczul, Maria and Gloria (unmarried daughters); Alberto, the eldest Maczul son, and his wife and three children; the second-eldest son and his wife and five children; and the eldest daughter and her husband and three children (their room was directly across from mine in the courtyard). The total number of people living in the house was twenty-two!

The Maczul family was considered one of the leading families in Patzún. Father Maczul was a successful farmer; he owned 100 *manzanas* of land five kilometers from town. (A manzana equals 0.7 hectares, or 1.7 acres. A family farm of 64 manzanas or larger, to be cultivated properly, requires the labor of a multifamily unit or of additional hired workers. Thus, the Maczul farm of 100 manzanas was considered a sizable inheritance.) Father Maczul, his sons, and his one son-in-law cultivated the Maczul farm with corn and beans. Although the family inheritance system in Patzún is considered patrilineal (as compared with the Ladino system in Zaragoza, which is bilateral), I had found that the growing land scarcity caused farmers not to divide their land, but rather to cultivate their farms cooperatively with all members of their families.

It seemed that the second son was the most energetic and his father's favorite. The eldest daughter appeared to have married rather poorly, as her husband always seemed to have been the brunt of jokes and was put to doing lesser chores. In fact, in a patrilineal society it is customary for married daughters to move into the household of *their husband's* family, rather than to remain in the household of their family of origin. However, cultural rules are broken from time to time, and in seeking to understand these variations, one usually finds that there are cultural rules to break the cultural rules. The exact reason as to why the Maczuls' eldest daughter remained living in her father's home is unknown, but perhaps the rule was broken in order that the Maczul family could

The Maczuls' eldest daughter and inquisitive infant in a rebozo

take advantage of having a son-in-law fulfill the lower-status role of doing the menial tasks. As in many societies people of higher income and status in the community may be allowed to break certain cultural rules for their own advantage.

Mother Maczul had the greatest power of all; with a flick of her hand her daughters-in-law and grandchildren fetched her anything she asked for. She appeared to love this type of attention, wearing a small smile on her face when people bowed to her commands or when they genuflected as she entered the room. I am not certain whether this practice of genuflecting is common in other towns, but it is a common practice among the larger families that live in Patzún. I believe it is a mark of the superior status of the eldest mother in a household of several mothers. A yellow ribbon braided within Mother Maczul's thick, black braids (she did not have any gray hair) signified that she was postmenopausal, thus deserving of reverence and respect. She had supposedly carried her burden long enough, and now she and her friends wore these ribbons of distinction quite proudly, walking wherever they wished and also claiming the best spots in the market from which to sell their weavings and wares.

The Maczul compound household was always lively; each night had seemed to bring activity, talking, singing, and moving about. I felt comfortable with this family. They all spoke some Spanish (although Cakchiquel was definitely the language of heart and hearth). Why then should I be struck with homesickness in such a lively, friendly place? I didn't know. Perhaps it was the sense of family and of my being an outsider, or perhaps I just missed my own home and the comforts of my own kitchen. Whatever the reasons, on one particular Sunday, I was miserable.

The four households each had their own kitchens, or rather they each had a corner of the compound where they prepared their meals. The eldest daughter did most of the cooking for the mother and father; I usually ate with them. The typical lunch was a type of vegetable soup or stew, bread, rice, and, during the rainy season, papayas or pineapples. Supper consisted of rice, black beans, and tortillas. This meal was similar to what I prepared in my own Zaragoza kitchen. The Indians didn't seem to eat differently from the Ladinos; no meals were elaborate, and food was not plentiful.

I had now been eating these same meals for almost four months, when one Sunday, remembering my own mother's cooking, I had an uncontrollable urge for a piece of lemon meringue pie. Desire for lemon pie popped out of my head and into my stomach and simply would not leave. I thought how much I hated beans and rice; what a stupid, inadequate diet! Bemoaning my plight, I tried to explain my frustration to Mother Maczul, who had what seemed to me, in this state of homesickness, a silly smile on her face. I said, in English, "I would gladly pay $500 for a piece of lemon meringue pie!" Of course, no one paid any attention to me. Thinking that I would simply die without this dessert, I got into my car and drove thirty miles to the home of my friend Edith, the British midwife. She was glad to see me, and upon hearing my misery, she said, "I'll fix that" and went about preparing the dessert. She produced a rolling pin made from a 7-Up bottle, squeezed juice from several limes that grew on vines along her fence, whipped up the meringue using a dinner fork, and proceeded to make and bake a marvelous *lemon meringue pie.* The object of my yearning, my dreams. Laughing as I wrote my field notes that night, I knew that I had experienced a predictable case of culture shock.

Culture shock usually has its peak between the eighth and twelfth month in the field, when both cultures—the one left and the one entered—compete in one's thinking and emotions. The "cure" is important, as such a shock can be so severe that a person will simply return home before his or her work is done. What to do when such an overwhelming shock sets in? Seek support—talk to friends. If possible, reestablish some of the old cultural structure again. In my case what worked was eating that lemon meringue pie. It was my past linked with my present. I was not alone in a strange world.

A Fight for Survival

I was still laughing about this incident as I neared the outskirts of Antigua. I had studied Spanish in Antigua, so I loved to drive the forty-five kilometers from my Zaragoza home to see old friends, to buy a few kitchen supplies, and, if I was really lucky, to take in a movie (which was usually several years old by the time it reached Antigua). This day was not going to allow such a dalliance. When I entered a favorite store to buy cheese and butter, the clerk, recognizing me, said, "I'm surprised to see you here. Aren't you worried about the hurricane?"

Startled to hear of his concern, I replied, "I didn't know that it would hit this far into the interior."

"It will cover the whole of Guatemala in just a few hours. Haven't you been listening to the local news?"

"Most of the time I can't get the news on my radio. I've never been in a hurricane before. What should I expect?"

"Hang on to everything! And don't go outside. I'm closing my store in just a few minutes. I heard from the capital that the winds were about 130 miles an hour and that means windows will break. It should hit within the hour," he said, in a worried voice, as he went about putting up shutters on the windows.

Now I knew why the streets were deserted! It was not, as I had been thinking, just an early-morning, peaceful moment. I hurried quickly to several other stores and heard the same prediction. As quickly as I could, I got into my car. Noticing that I only had a half-tank of gasoline, I decided to stop at a gasoline station. Several were already closed; fortunately, one was still open. As the attendant filled up the tank, he said, "You had better take cover right away." I knew that I still had forty-four kilometers of rough driving to do before I could.

The sky was now a darker green, and the winds were beginning to wail. I could feel the heaviness of the clouds as I pointed the car back to Zaragoza and up the mountainside. My mind didn't wander to lemon pies this time. I fought bravely the increasing winds; a few sprinkles gave warning of what was to come. I drove the next thirty-four kilometers without a problem. With ten kilometers still to go, the tall corn began to lean and sway. There were no houses along this route, only a few scattered cane huts. I realized that I knew no one living between Zaragoza and Antigua—most of the road traveled through cornfields, with few or no houses along the way. The drive to Antigua had always seemed so short, quick, and familiar, but now it felt a dangerous fiend. The rain soon came in sheets of blinding force. With my nose on the windshield, I fought to see the narrow white lines that marked the edges of the road and the beginning of the deep ravines on either side. Up and down the hills and valleys I flew, as fast as it was safe. At last I saw the flat valley of Zaragoza and the gleaming-white cemetery tombs. Creeping down toward the cathedral, I let the ruts of the road lead me to my parking place in the churchyard. I grasped my sack of food and fought the wind and rain, as I ran to my house. It took all of my strength to stand erect, and when I finally opened the door of my house, a sheet of rain entered along with me.

Finding a Friend—Muñeca

The only sound I could hear was the howling wind. The electricity was gone. Lighting several candles, I fought the darkness and my own fear. How I had wished Silvia and Pablo were next door! I knew they'd be my support and comfort. Several times during the night, I had thought that my tin roof would be torn away, as the winds had grown increasingly stronger. Water had entered every room in my house, nothing would stop it. The night was long and lonely. I took refuge in my cot, keeping warm in my sleeping bag but hoping that the water wouldn't rise to the level of my bed. It didn't, and morning finally came, but late, for the darkness remained. The rains appeared to be lessening—or was it to be the eye of the storm? I was thankful that my window was small and barred with steel. At one point, the rain and wind became so light that I decided to peek outside. There was no one on the street—only the quietness that occurs after a disaster. Then I saw it—a small, gray bundle outside in the gutter. What was it? A rat or a child? No, it was a dog! I looked again and wondered whether it had drowned? Perhaps we were the only living creatures left, I thought. I went outside to investigate. It was alive, the poor skeleton of a thing. With the rain pouring on both of us, I picked up the bundle of bones and brought it into my house. Its eyes were dull; this creature looked nearly dead.

That's how I got my dog, Muñeca (doll—named after my dog at home). The first day, I was sure that Muñeca would not survive— she was so weak and hungry. I could see each bone of her gray body. Her first meal came out as pure mud feces. I guessed that the only meal she had eaten in a long time must have been dirt. As the days went by, the rains ceased and the sun came out again. Muñeca grew fat with my good care, and her coat changed from a dull gray to a glossy, beautiful golden brown. She was the pet of the town, as she went everywhere with me. The farmers, already poverty stricken, weren't as lucky as Muñeca; their crops had been ruined. The full-kerneled heads of corn had been swept into the mud and water. We worried that some people would starve. Those who had saved some corn from the preceding year were able to plant for the next season, but that year everyone was hungry.

I had learned the ways of the people as a result of the hurricane. Their answer to most disasters was quite simple: It's God's will. Life had its meaning in the pattern of giving and taking, and people with so little to begin with had so little to lose. They just picked up where things left off and began the cycle of living again. On the other hand, the next disaster, Volcano Fuego, was not so easily understood.

Chapter 14

Volcano Fuego
Rims of Fire and Witchery

> My commitment to our struggle recognizes neither boundaries
> nor limits: only those of us who carry our cause in our hearts
> are willing to run the risks.
> —Rigoberta Menchú, *I, Rigoberta Menchú: An Indian Woman
> in Guatemala*, 1992

It was now a couple of months after Hurricane Fifi; life was going on as usual. The household survey was moving along—slowly, as expected, but without major problems. I continued to stay with the Maczul family in Patzún as well as to live in my house in Zaragoza. My husband had returned to the States to finish his dissertation. The children would come for visits from Huehuetenango about once a month, and I would visit them in between those times. I had the fieldwork pretty much down to a routine, and I could begin to see finishing the data collection in time to return to the University of Colorado, where I would analyze the survey data and our children could enroll, at home in Colorado, for classes in the spring. I planned on returning to Zaragoza and Patzún for several of months in the summer of 1975, after the fertility data were analyzed, so that I might interpret and synthesize all the findings, as well as make any last observations I felt would be important for my dissertation.

A Smoking Giant Speaks

The dry season began; the days and nights were crisp. Upon waking in the morning, it was refreshing to walk outside and gaze at Volcano Fuego, just ten kilometers south of Zaragoza. Its cone was nearly perfect, and now and then a wisp of white smoke would rise from it. Occasionally there were trails of black smoke, but nothing of consequence. I asked Silvia if she had ever seen it erupt during her seventy years. "Yes, about fifteen years ago there was a large eruption that lasted about two days," she replied. "It just let off some steam."

I had gone to bed at my usual time, about 10:30, when suddenly I heard a roar, which grew louder and louder, until it finally sounded like five or six jet planes just outside my door. What could it be? I thought. Then the room began to wave and shift, as if the ground were Jello. I was sure it was an earthquake. I got up and ran to the door, thinking that the doorway was the safest place in which to stand. Then I looked outside. There I saw an incredible sight. Volcano Fuego was erupting! As tall as the volcano was, flames were shooting up twice as high. The width of the eruption was as broad as the whole volcano. I felt as if I were witness to Mount Olympus, with Zeus about to speak.

Several neighbors had also come out of their houses. I didn't feel in danger, only fascinated with the display of power. Then I saw flashes of lightning crossing the ground in front of me and in between the buildings: it traveled toward the church and the school and then across toward the market and the Município. Lightning was everywhere. One of my neighbors shouted, "Get back inside your house! The lightning is dangerous!" The streets were deserted. I hurried in but felt conflicted, because I wanted to take photographs of this monumental event. However, remembering to follow the lead of my neighbors, I stayed inside all night.

It was hard to sleep, as the roar continued, though it lessened toward morning. As I got out of bed, I noticed something more strange; it had become very, very cold during the night. The energy force must have created a reversal of heat fields, because the tip of Fuego appeared covered with *ice and snow*. Yet the lightning was still flashing around the cone, and I could hear thunder. I paused to wonder if this could have been how the Ice Ages began—with heavy volcanic activity and the reversal of energy fields from hot to cold. I didn't have much time to ponder; I had to work quickly like my neighbors. We cleared the ash off our rooftops with brooms and hosed them with water, because the heaviness of the ash, they told me, would cause the roof to crash in. Several roofs had already done so, I was told. We were living through danger, as we went about quietly, always looking over our shoulders at the continuing eruption of Fuego.

We had been told that among the Indians who lived close to the cone, seven had been killed and about twenty-five of them had lost their homes to the cinders and volcanic ash. They had fled to Zaragoza, the closest town. Shelters of tents and boxes were set up for them in the plaza, and we were asked for donations. We all gave, grateful to have our homes safe for the time being. Zaragoza had the reputation of being a town where Indians never entered—and if they did, they needed to leave before sundown. I remembered a night when Magdelena had come to my home for supper, and she was very nervous about staying after sundown. Other than her anxiety and the town's reputation, I had never seen any evidence of discrimination. But there were never any Indians in town. That may seem strange in a department where the majority are Indian; however, there are many roads around Zaragoza. If one wants to avoid coming into the town it is quite possible.

Now there were more than twenty Indians taking shelter in the town. What would happen? Although rumors continued, I never saw discrimination during this time of disaster. I even went out with my neighbors on a couple of occasions to take food to the victims. The people of Zaragoza were very generous, helping the victims with food and shelter for over three weeks. When the roads were cleared, the Indians simply returned to their homes, their customary way of handling losses and disasters.

The Giant Is Not a Good Neighbor

Unfortunately, Fuego was not a good neighbor, and it continued to erupt for over two months. It wasn't pleasant; in fact, it grew to be disgusting. The streets were constantly full of slick, greasy volcanic ash. To drive in it was like trying to drive on streets covered with lard. The rooftops were a mess; they needed to be hosed down every morning. The first time had been rewarding, as we were bonded in the press to save our homes. But hosing down a rooftop on a daily basis grows wearying. We also needed to wear face masks in order to breathe. People developed all kinds of illnesses, due in part to the stifling, dusty air. I had terrible sinus headaches, and my eyes itched constantly.

"What causes the volcano to erupt?" I asked Silvia.

"There is a serpent who lives under the mountain," she replied. "Every now and then he gets very upset and angry. Maybe we haven't been kind to one another, or we have cheated, or have been jealous. Sometimes we don't know what we have done, but he [the serpent] gets very angry. Then he opens up his mouth and out comes the fire and smoke." I was dismayed to learn that a rational woman, like my businesswoman mother, could possibly believe such an explanation, but accepting it as her value and part of her belief system, I did not argue.

I found that the patzuñeros also shared a similar belief about a serpent under the mountain. "How do you get the anger to change? How do you get him to stop belching up smoke and fire?" I asked them.

"You have to be good to your neighbors and your family," they answered. "You have to confess your sins."

I knew there probably were other things that needed to be done to appease the serpent, but I couldn't put my finger on it. The day after the first eruption, I noticed that a bucket of water had been placed by my doorway. I thought that someone had accidentally forgotten it, but I wondered, too, if it had something to do with the volcanic ash. Several days later I found a small pile of three stones in my living room. Obviously, someone had been coming into my house when I wasn't there. I decided to observe for a while, before investigating further. After a couple of weeks, I discovered that several of the peach trees in my backyard had pieces of fruit and candy tied onto their branches. More stones had been piled in a triangle near my pila and a photograph of the Virgin Mary had been tied onto a branch of a bush near the pila. I realized that I had become part of some system of dewitching. I remembered the brujo of Xajáxac and the use of dogs for revenge. I kept an eye on Muñeca, and I inspected my car for signs of tampering. I found none, but I thought it was time to discuss these actions with my mother. I was sure she was the visitor who was introducing these items, since she was the only other person who had a key to my house. So I asked her.

"I'm trying to protect you," Silvia said simply. "These are the ways of our people." I could tell that she didn't want to discuss these ways any further; perhaps she felt that by discussing them, she would deplete them of their power. I knew she was trustworthy, so I stopped questioning.

We all grew terribly weary of Fuego. Nothing seemed to stop the eruption. Most of the time it was slight, but irritating; occasionally the eruption would be strong. We all wished that she (everyone called the volcano "she," perhaps to neutralize the "male" serpent inside—a yin and yang balance?) would quiet down. People in the town grew ill-tempered—I could feel the tension. There were no dances, no fun-loving sports on the weekends, no serenading at the windows; the only event that took place was the monotonous cleaning of the rooftops.

I had begun to accept the constant headache and squishy driving as two of the irritants of living in a subtropical, volcanic land. However, one weekend, when my children had come to spend a couple of days with me, I began to feel very, very uneasy. Around noontime, the feeling was overwhelming. I took this as a foreboding sign, a forewarning, similar to that "we just know" explanation, the people had often given me. I couldn't tell the children about what exactly was bothering me, because I didn't know. I simply felt that we were in some unexplainable danger.

A Peaceful Retreat and a Surprise Visit

Suddenly I said, "Let's go to the lake [Lake Atitlán]." I recalled our friend, Dr. Eugénio Schieber, saying, "Come whenever you want; the cabin is usually empty, just check with the gardener who lives next door, and he will let you in." Paul and Janis were ecstatic. It was fun to go to Lake Atitlán at any time of year. The beaches were beautiful, and there were places to explore. It would be especially nice to be away from the heavy volcanic ash. We loaded the car within ten minutes and were soon driving down the Pan-American Highway. It wasn't an easy trip, about three hours on winding mountain roads, but it was worth it.

Once we reached the lake, I knew I had made the right decision. Lake Atitlán—a vision of crystal-clear, blue waters rimmed with volcanoes on three sides—is one of the world's most beautiful sights. It is a mysterious lake that is quiet and blue in the early-morning hours and at night, but during the middle of the day, the rising heat causes currents of air to circulate between the volcanoes and stir the waters into gigantic, churning gray waves creating a *chukamul*, the Mayan word for whirlpool. The natives refused to cross the lake at midday for fear of being swept under by the large whirlpool. During that time it is wise to sit and watch the forces of nature once again.

Sleep came easy that night. We were safe, together, and breathing the clear mountain air. We awakened the next morning with unbounded energy. We all took long morning swims and enjoyed a late breakfast; later we took one more swim. "We need to leave soon so you can catch your bus back to Huehuetenango tomorrow morning," I called, swimming toward the shore. "Yeah, we know, Mom," they responded, disappointed.

As I was about a half-mile from the shore, I glanced toward the pier and thought my eyes had deceived me; for on the beach appeared to be seven men who looked strangely familiar. They were town councilmen from Zaragoza! What were they doing here? I

Mysterious, majestic Lake Atitlán—a refuge and retreat

swam to shore, put a towel around myself, and went to greet them.

"How nice to see you, but also a surprise," I said.

They greeted me in like manner.

"Would you like some coffee?" I asked.

"Yes, thank you."

I fixed coffee and served cookies, and we chatted about the beautiful day. I explained that we were about to return to Zaragoza and asked if any would like a ride back. Yes, they all would. I explained that the car was pretty small and in these mountains, we could only take three of them with the children and myself. Even with the reduced number, it was a slow trip back, and the car overheated several times, causing us to have to stop and wait until it cooled down. At last we reached Chimaltenango, where I needed to run some errands before going home. All the men had things to do too and so got out as well. After doing a little shopping, the children and I stopped to see my friend Edith in her small apartment.

A Murder or a Sacrifice?

As soon as Edith opened the door, she grabbed me and hugged me tightly, "Jody, Jody, I'm so glad to see you alive! We were all worried about you!" she exclaimed. "Are you all right? Where did you go?"

I was dumbfounded. Why was she so overjoyed to see us?

"Maybe you don't know what happened? Have you heard about the murder?"

"No, we were at the lake. Who was murdered?"

"Thelma, the American nurse!"

"Oh, no! Tell us about it," I cried.

Edith began to explain. "It seems that since Fuego hasn't been letting up, some of the people were worried that there was some black magic going on—something that could explain why it was still erupting after all this time. You know Thelma lived alone. [Thelma was an American who had lived in Zaragoza for about twenty years, but she was still considered an outsider.] And she had this awful skin cancer. You know what fair-complexioned people get in this equatorial sun. She looked awful with all of those sores on her face. Some of the natives think that nurses have special power, or may even be witches. So apparently four men armed themselves with clubs and went over to Thelma's house last night and beat her to death. They even beat and killed her little dog. I guess they thought he was evil, too."

I gasped, thinking of my own dog and my own reputation as an outsider—and also what my mother had told me about the serpent being angry. I thought about the dewitching evidence I had seen placed around my house. I hadn't known my life, and perhaps the children's, had been so endangered.

Edith continued, "They caught the four men yesterday, just a block from your house. We heard that the police were worried that these men were coming to kill you, too, as Fuego was still erupting this morning!"

I was shaking as I recalled the urgency that I had felt when the children and I had left for the lake. Then this morning when the town councilmen had come to visit me, they kept saying, "Everything is OK in Zaragoza. You are safe here; we're so glad you came." I believed that they had come to see if I were still alive and to let me know that they were my protectors.

"Where are the killers now?" I asked shakily.

"They're in prison, right here in Chimaltenango. You know here in Guatemala it's the Napoleonic law: you are guilty until proven innocent. I hear that they received life sentences."

I wondered. To people without resources to understand the workings of nature, no doubt their explanation was as good as any. I was glad that the children and I had been spared any kind of confrontation with their solution. I talked this situation over with my mother as best I could. She was glad to see us, pouring holy water over our heads and saying prayers for about fifteen minutes. Next I went to the mayor's office to greet him and to tell him how grateful I was to live in a town like Zaragoza. As I walked from the municipal building to my house, the shadows were growing long. I looked up at Fuego, beautiful against the evening sky, and for the first time in nearly two months, it stood unbelievably silent. There was no smoke, no fire. Perhaps the gods (or the serpent) had, indeed, been appeased!

I thought I would talk with my friends back in Patzún, to see whether they had similar thoughts and perhaps similar ways to purify me.

Chapter 15

Folk Ideologies
The Miracles and Myths of Maximón

> So human societies, left to themselves, will select parts of their heritage for elaboration, and the original choice will gain in impetus from generation to generation until a coherent individual culture has been developed.
> —Margaret Mead, *Dominant Cultural Attitudes in Manu'a,* 1959

The days following the murder of the American nurse in Zaragoza and my own lucky escape left me pondering how I was to learn more about the folk or traditional ideologies present in both towns. What was happening around me that I wasn't aware of? The people in Zaragoza and Patzún obviously had traditional religions that helped explain and alleviate anxieties about the unknown—those events that occurred without an apparent cause—and without an apparent solution. When people told me that the eruption of Volcano Fuego was caused by an underground serpent spewing out fire now and then, I wondered how the explanation fit within their larger belief system about the cosmos, or, in other words, their ideology. Also the suspicious things I had found around my house in Zaragoza indicated to me that the townspeople, particularly my fictive mother, Silvia, must have been worried either about my magical powers or the magical powers aimed at harming me.

Being Part of a Magical World

Part of me wanted to ignore this nonshared magical world. On the other hand, I knew that I was somehow also a part of it and needed to at least be aware of how this ideology fit within the cultural system I was studying. How could I tap into the folk religion and go beyond merely attending masses and ritual ceremonies, such as baptisms, weddings, and funerals? As an outsider, studying the ideologies of a group would be difficult, for it would bring me face to face with the differences between "we" and "they," between the in-group and the out-group. Ideologies are closely held beliefs, developed over long periods of time. They serve to maintain an evolving, adapting, and surviving social group. Legends and myths perpetuate ideologies; they explain how the universe works and how humans interact with and struggle with the environment. The interpretations of the supernatural form the substance of folk religions or ideologies.

I knew that the spiritual world was real for both the Ladino and the Indian, as they would talk about their ancestors' spirits as if they were present and an element of aid or help in time of trouble. Silvia once said, "When I need her, my mother is here; she comes to give me advice, to comfort me."

"You mean, her *espíritu* [spirit]?" I asked.

"Yes, her spirit is here. There are other spirits as well; some are good and others are bad."

"How can you tell the difference? Do you see them?" I continued questioning.

"No, you can't see them, but you can feel them; you can feel when they are in a room with you. You can feel when they are in the street or around you," she answered. "Good spirits are light, they are happy; bad ones are dark and bring you feelings of sadness, fear, or foreboding, as though something bad is going to happen."

"Does it help to talk with the priest; does he get rid of the bad ones?"

"Some priests are very powerful and can get rid of bad spirits, in your body or in your home or in other places, too. Padre Pius doesn't do much of that; he stays in the cathedral, but Hermana [Sister] Marta [one of the Guatemalan nuns in the convent] knows how to anoint and give you prayers for healing."

Having heard of this healing power, I went to the convent across the street from me to visit Hermana Marta. She lived with five other nuns; all were from Guatemala and of a different order from the American nuns of San Bernandino. Hermana Marta was about thirty-five years old, about five-feet-two-inches tall, and very dark complexioned. Her eyes were a flashing, dark-brown color; her smile was soft and tentative. She spoke in a very quiet, slow manner. We sat at a sturdy wooden table in the middle of a sparsely furnished *sala* (living room) in the convent, and Hermana Marta explained her belief in spirits to me. "I know that most of the people in Zaragoza believe in spirits, and I do, too, but I don't believe in some of the legends of the naturales; they carry such ancient beliefs around, even in today's world. I use simple prayers from our many saints of the Catholic church—prayers I give for the sick. I believe in miracles, but only of the kind that God sends, not other spirits. When I pray for the sick, I use an oil to anoint their heads, just as was done during the time of Jesus, but I don't use any magical potions as some of the naturales do. They also sacrifice chickens, especially roosters, and use the blood for various ceremonies. If a person is very sick, I go to their home, but mostly people come to the cathedral, where I have prayer intercessions for them. Most of the time, the priest does such ceremonies, but here, in this parish, Padre Pius doesn't have the time to hold these services, so I have been the one to do them—although it is unusual for a nun to do the prayer service."

While I knew that it was important to discuss the folk religion with Hermana Marta, I also knew that she was part of a formalized religion and really didn't represent the folk, traditional religion found in the surrounding villages and hamlets such as I had seen practiced by the brujo in Xajáxac several years earlier. I needed to talk more with the Indians in Patzún to learn their story.

In the weeks that followed I spent time with my fictive sister Maria in Patzún, talking about the Indian folk practices in religion. She seemed less eager to talk about these things than about other subjects, such as selling corn in the market or wedding ceremonies. I knew she feared giving away secrets, and thus allowing these practices to lose some of their power, by giving information to me. "We have several sacred caves where we go to have special ceremonies; here we have some sacrifices of chickens, prayers for special things, and sometimes requests for healing or for revenge," Maria revealed in response to one of my questions.

"I'd like to go with you sometime to participate in a ceremony," I offered eagerly.

"These are special celebrations for Indians, and I'm afraid the people wouldn't welcome an outsider," Maria answered honestly and directly. I felt she was right; maybe if I were to be here many more years, I would be invited, but now I was still a stranger.

"You might want to come with me to the shrine for Hermano [Brother] Maximón; even gringos can go into his shrine. There are many shrines around Guatemala, but the closest is in San Andrés Itzapa, a village nearby."

"I would like, very much, to go to the shrine. When can we go?" I asked quickly.

Folk Catholicism, a mixture of indigenous and Western rituals and ceremonies

"Let's go next Sunday. The shrine will be filled with people coming from the City, and you will see many interesting things. You will be able to see all of the many types of people who believe in his power and his miracles," Maria added.

"Good," I replied, "I will be here early on Sunday, and we'll drive over."

I had read about Hermano Maximón (Gaitán, 1976) and had heard an occasional remark about him from my neighbors, but I did not know there was a shrine nearby. I wanted to learn more about the miracles performed in the shrine and how they fit within the ideology of the group.

Maximón is called by several names—Hermano Maximón, San Simón, Hermano Simón—but all basically refer to an Indian saint. The actual origin of the legend of Maximón is difficult to trace, but it seems the stories about the life and miracles of this saint arose about 100 years ago throughout the Indian population in Central and South America. Writers believe that the Indians, being a marginal people without much power, built a belief about a protector—one who, like them, was mortal, with mortal desires, beliefs, and actions. In this new saint, the Indians found a powerful helper who did not discriminate against them. Maximón is not recognized as a saint by the Catholic church, as he represents the sinful Christian. In fact, in many writings, Maximón is also called Judas Iscariot, the disciple who betrayed Jesus for thirty coins and who is known throughout the Catholic world as one of the most sinful of beings. I was told by several Indians that it is the sinful nature of Maximón that attracts fellow transgressors—those who lie and cheat, drink booze, and who want wealth, good luck, and good health. Thus, according to my Indian informants, Maximón represents the sinners of the world. For this reason, the Indians and others believe they can approach an understanding saint to ask for favors and protection.

Visiting Maximón at San Andrés Itzapa

On Sunday, as planned, Maria and I drove to San Andrés Itzapa, a town about ten kilometers from Patzún. It, too, is an Indian town, but a bit smaller than Patzún. As we drove into the town's center, we saw approximately fifteen cars lining the streets. "That's near the shrine; you can see how many people drive from such long distances just to see San Simón, to pray, and to light some candles," Maria explained. "Why not park here. We can walk over to the shrine and on the way buy some candles ourselves."

Magic candles and cigars for Brother Maximón

We walked over the cobblestone streets, and as we neared the shrine, I saw numerous vendors on the sidewalk, selling statues of various sizes of the Indian saint, photographs, souvenirs, incense, and candles. We ducked into a shop along the sidewalk that was filled with more items of worship for Maximón. The most popular item seemed to be candles—of all sizes and several colors.

"What are the different colors for?" I asked.

"Each one is for a special request, a particular prayer," Maria replied. "For instance, the green one is for wealth, for good crops; the white one is to protect people, mostly children, who are pure and innocent; the red one, of course, is for love, romance, and marriage. The blue one is for justice and truth; the yellow is for protection for the "little" people—those who don't have protection, such as widows, old people, and marginal folks [those like the Hernández and Caj families who had few resources and no power base or family or institutions to help them survive; those who remained outside the mainstream of life]. The black one is for giving bad luck, but also for protecting from bad luck. It is really powerful; you must be careful when you use that one!"

I also noticed some small bottles filled with liquor and boxes filled with cigars. "What are those things used for?" I asked.

"Because our Hermano is just like us; he likes to smoke cigars and to drink alcohol. Those bottles and cigars are gifts to be given to him." We bought several bottles, a few cigars, and candles of all colors. Then we walked toward the shrine.

We crossed a large plaza where more vendors were selling their worship items. Then we entered the shrine. I was surprised how dark it was inside; there were no lights except for the glow from the burning candles. There must have been several hundred lighted candles on the flat tablelike structure, which stood at about eye level for most Indians. The smell of incense filled the room. I noticed candles of every color on the table. I lit a red one, for love. Maria lit a blue one—so that the truth she was telling me would be heard correctly and so there wouldn't be any confusion to be blamed on her, I guessed. I saw several very large black candles and wondered who would be the recipient of the bad luck (or have it warded off with the special protective powers).

There were about fifty people in line to see the statue of Maximón. The image of the Indian saint was placed upright on a large chair, resembling a throne. I had seen photographs of the saint in a book, but was still surprised to see "in person" this legendary saint. The statue was life-sized, closed in by glass on three sides. The enclosure was filled with flowers and satin bunting. Without meaning to appear irreverent, to me he looked like an Italian organ grinder—

at least like those I have seen in photographs. He had a thin black mustache; he was dressed in a black hat, a dark, expensive-looking suit, a white shirt, and a striped necktie. His chalk-white face was thin, not like the broad Indian face, and his black eyes were large and serious looking, and stared straight ahead. His shoes were shiny black patent leather. He looked nothing like an Indian, in dress or in facial features.

"I guess I thought that Maximón would look like a Mayan person, if he is your brother. Do you know the reason he looks so different?" I asked Maria in a soft, but puzzled way.

"I don't know, I guess we just like him that way," was her reply.

Often a fieldworker finds that the history of a legend or myth is lost, and only the artifact, such as the statue of Maximón, remains. In the minds of the people, it has always been that way. Sometimes, through further research, a plausible history can be found, but sometimes a fieldworker just must accept the face value of a certain belief or practice—it just is.

"It is also a mystery about how he is dressed. He has several changes of clothes; sometimes he is dressed like a general, with braid and ribbons, as if he has been in battles. Or Hermano may be in a khaki uniform, just like an ordinary soldier. The president of the Republic once said that San Simón had more neckties than he did! How he changes these clothes, no one knows; it just happens!" remarked Maria.

I didn't go up the steps to the shrine, but Maria did, and left the cigars and liquor there. I would intrude in the worship of these followers if I approached the statue itself, so I watched the details. Each petitioner slowly walked forward and up the steps to the chair/throne. As the person reached the throne, an assistant, a woman standing by the statue, helped the petitioner. The petitioner would talk with the assistant, then put money, cigars, liquor, and/or tortillas on the lap of San Simón or on the satin bunting surrounding the statue. Then the assistant would sprinkle water on the head, shoulders, and back of the petitioner (she would actually touch some of them). Sometimes the assistant would bend over backward, praying loudly as she did. Many petitioners stared into space; others were crying as they walked down the steps on the other side. Some held up their children, presumably for blessings. Some prayed out loud. The atmosphere was reverent, as in church.

We stayed about a half-hour; I took some photographs—Maria said it would be OK. Written on the wall was a prayer that caught my attention and touched my heart:

> O powerful San Simón, I am a humble creature; be with me. Aid
> me in all my acts and protect me from danger. Evil spirits will
> leave me if I say your name. I offer you cigars, tortillas, liquor
> and candles, for you are my brother.

I noticed another prayer was written in the familiar *tu* form of the
Spanish word for *you*:

> Brother, Brother, you who suffered so much, I, a poor person,
> ask you for good crops and food for my children. You have
> suffered the same as we have; you know that we need water and
> bread for life. Please help me.

These prayers and what I saw at the shrine helped me to understand
the need the Indians had for a saint of their own—one who was at
their level but also one who could help them deal with life with a
bit of humor and perhaps fantasy.

As we walked away, I could tell that Maria was pleased that she
had brought me. I felt that I had learned something more about the
hoe-and-machete people who lived with danger and risks, gambles
and losses every day. I respected their need for a saint who didn't
discriminate against them. Maria knew that I understood and
empathized with them. This was not true of one of my colleagues,
however.

The Adventure of an Irreverent Professor

After I drove Maria back to Patzún, I went to Chimaltenango to
join some of my American friends for supper. I told them about my
experience at the shrine and the meaning it had for me. Ed, a college
professor from the United States, who had been passing through
on his summer vacation, had remarked, "I would really like to see
that shrine. Why don't you take me there, too."

"I guess it would be okay," I replied. "We could go next Sunday
if you'd like."

"Great! I'll meet you at your house in Zaragoza," Ed said.

The week went by, and Ed drove to my house. With him was
another American, Pete. I explained to them that it was important
to be respectful of the Indians' worship and to stay in the
background. They agreed that this was their intention. As we
entered San Andrés, they wanted to buy candles, just as I had.
When they saw the array, I explained the use of each different color.
Ed said, "Oh, I know a department chairman I'd like to fix! I want
that big black one," he laughed loudly. Both Pete and I said we
didn't think that was a good idea, as the candles were not to be

misused. Instead of listening, Ed bought the largest black candle in the shop. I felt uncomfortable as we walked into the shrine. Again the darkness, except for the candles, was striking. I stood back as Ed lit the large black candle and placed it among the many colored ones that filled the table. We stayed, again for a half-hour, then left. Ed and Pete didn't stay for coffee at my Zaragoza house, as it was getting dark and they wanted to return to Antigua for supper that night.

I thought little more about the incident until I saw Ed two days later at the telegraph office in Chimaltenango. His face was scratched, and his arm had a large bandage on it. "What happened to you?" I asked.

"I had an accident Sunday night as we returned to Antigua," Ed replied with a tense look on his face. "It was the weirdest thing I've ever experienced," he continued. "Remember that black candle I lit in the shrine? Well, I think it really was bad luck. I shouldn't have done it.

"As we were rounding one of the turns on the highway to Antigua, a black dog came running out of the bushes and crossed in front of my car. I was startled and tried to avoid hitting him, but instead I lost control of my car, and it started toward a ditch. We went in—thank goodness it was a shallow ditch!—but we went into a spin. I swear that as the car began to turn over, the black dog that had run in front of my car turned into San Simón. I know it sounds crazy, but Pete saw it, too; the dog actually looked like San Simón. His face, even with the black mustache, was right in my windshield. The car went over on its top and just stopped there with the wheels straight up. The top was smashed down almost to the seat. Pete and I could hardly crawl out. I had cuts on my head and on my arm, but Pete wasn't hurt at all. As we looked at my upside-down car, we wondered how we were ever going to get it out of the ditch and on its wheels again. Just then a large truck came by and in the back were twelve men dressed in purple robes and wearing those pointed, tall hats—those that you see in religious processions. Well, these twelve men jumped out of the truck without saying a word, lifted up my car and turned it on its wheels again. They jumped back into the truck without ever saying a word. Pete and I were dumbfounded. We just got back into the car. Of course, the top was so smashed down that we could hardly get in—the roof had been crunched nearly to the level of the steering wheel—but we managed to slide into the seats anyway. The car started up, so I drove away. I was shaking so badly, I nearly went off the road again, but we finally got back to Antigua. The car is getting fixed now. That's how I scratched my face and my arm. Not bad, but I know it really did happen!" Ed's face was as white as a sheet as he described in detail his most amazing story.

"Wow," I said. "I've never heard such a weird tale before. I guess it tells us something about breaking the cultural rules, even if we don't understand what it all means."

"You're right about that," replied Ed, shaking his head and still looking very tense.

Folk Heroes, Myths, and Legends

I never had a chance to return to the shrine of Maximón at San Andrés Itzapa, but I never forgot the story of Ed and his black candle, nor did I lose sight of the reverence I had experienced in such a brief span of time. I still recall the worshipers—their faces, the whispers, the gentle prayer written on the side of the wall, the smell of the candles and liquor. Belief systems are the foundations of cultures and permit humans to extend beyond their own mortal selves through whatever forms their worship may take.

I heard many stories about the miracles of San Simón. Some indicated that he made mysterious visits to homes to protect the occupants. Others told of deaths predicted by San Simón. Still others told of happy marriages and protected children, the result of his intercessions. In the Epilogue I tell another story of a miraculous event involving this folk hero-folk saint.

This exercise of participating in a worship service as a means of delving more deeply into the religion and ideology of a culture holds great potential for further study. It is an example of a critical part of the fieldwork that an anthropologist does. Careful listening to how the stories (legends, myths, folktales, and even jokes) are told by the people one is studying can reveal, in quite clear detail, the underlying social structure of that society. Some anthropologists spend their careers analyzing such artifacts as a means of comprehending the richness of a culture.

In reviewing the myths (stories told as true) about San Simón, one can understand more clearly the ideologies of the Indian people of Patzún and the surrounding area. But perhaps rather than trying to comprehend the minute details of these myths or folktales, it is more important to study the larger picture of how the belief in a saint—one who is so similar yet so powerful—meets the human need of having an ideology that shapes a sense of personal control over unpredictable life events. And there certainly are unpredictable events in the daily lives of both the Ladinos and the Indians I studied. Maximón, whether historically real or imagined, does bring a sense of peace, tranquility, and dignity to many people met in this ethnography.

Chapter 16

How Many Children Do We Want? And Why?

> You realize that living with only one culture, one way of doing things, is a prison. When you expand your perspective, some of the walls of your cultural prison will disappear.
> —Paul Bohannan, *We,The Alien*, 1992

I knew whole chunks of the puzzle were missing! Studying the folktales, myths, and legends were important to frame the fabric of the culture, to study the cognitive maps of the people. But I needed more.

Nagging, Unanswered Questions

I needed to get closer to the details of each community if I really wanted to compare them. I needed to see more clearly the patterns of childbearing in each community—the various forms and patterns of spacing children, of delaying pregnancies, and of terminating those that would be a deficit to the struggling family (just as I had seen in the home of the brujo with his dying grandson). I knew the nagging questions had no simple answers (I recalled the sorrow of the parents whose twelve-year-old son had died of lockjaw). And, especially now that I had experienced two natural disasters with the people, I understood that the margin for error was so small, and the governmental structure so frail, that there was no disaster relief, except that a family eat less. I also had experienced the oppression

173

wrought by a governmental official who, with a machine gun and an official stamp, destroyed the dreams of many. What could I now say about the patterns of childbearing? How could this ethnography lend better understanding to the question I first asked in the woods behind the Behrhorst Hospital after Baby Rosa died in her mother's arms: Why do poverty-stricken people have the number of children they do when half are destined to die? I needed to know the essentials—enough to interpret these cultures and predict their future course based on the fieldwork done thus far. If only I could sit down with each woman and man and discuss their beliefs and practices concerning childbearing, perhaps then I would understand. Such a solution was impractical; however, what could be done would be to conduct a household survey—to gather a representative sample of the thoughts, beliefs, and practices of the people in each town. And this is what I did, beginning in the fall of 1974.

The Household Fertility Survey

I knew I needed to do a household fertility study: to examine carefully the patterns of childbearing, to learn women's concerns about having and raising children. I decided to survey only women, knowing that men were often absent from Zaragoza, and believing that women knew the family's decision about reproduction. Doing such a detailed survey would lengthen my doctoral studies by at least six months—well into 1975. I could not do additional work without financial support. With gratitude I received a letter from my dissertation advisor, Dr. Smith, notifying me that I had been awarded a National Science Foundation dissertation research support grant of $1,800. I could use it for my fieldwork and data analysis. I was elated; with this support I could now afford to buy maps, prepare the questionnaires (in Spanish), and hire two indigenous interviewers to help me complete the long reproduction interviews with women. With additional money I could return to Colorado to analyze the data with the aid of a computer. After the data runs I could return again to the field to complete the ethnography. I immediately began developing a questionnaire. This reproductive history and family decision-making questionnaire was built on understanding the people's lifeways. If I had prepared the questionnaire upon first arriving, I would have missed many important concerns. The questionnaire focused on issues pertaining to zaragozaños and patzuñeros but could apply to other families living at subsistence levels in other peasant societies as well. This survey proved to strengthen and validate the ethnographic fieldwork.

The Questionnaire

Ethnographies do not always include questionnaires and household surveys. I will describe the rigor needed in this additional research method, as readers may want to know how the data were collected and just what data were included.

This questionnaire consisted of 204 items pertaining to the reproductive history of ever-mated women between the ages of fifteen and forty-nine (meaning they could become pregnant; they were fecund) and the demographic picture of the household (such items as years of education, literacy, economic status, religion, and migration histories). Data also were gathered about the ideals and values women held: about the numbers of children a family should have; their opinions about being women; aspirations for their children; their work role in the household; and their knowledge of, attitude toward, and practice of using modern contraceptives (the pill, the spiral, or the injection).

Items concerning the reproductive histories were the most detailed and included questions about the outcome of a pregnancy (full-term, miscarriage or abortion, stillbirth), name of the child, and whether he or she survived the first five years. Demographers use specific international measures for comparisons of fertility. A *fertility rate* refers to the incidence of births in a female population. Examples of fertility rates are crude birth rates, general birth rates, age-specific birth rates, and total fertility rates. The age-specific rate is the most valuable, as it excludes from the population those women not exposed to childbearing, such as those who are too young, too old, or otherwise not mating (widows, for instance). This rate expresses the probability that a woman of a specified age (for example, between twenty and twenty-four years) would bear a child within the year. The total fertility is a sum of all the age-specific fertility rates for the study's sample. As can readily be seen, having such data to compare childbearing patterns would help a researcher to solve the riddle of reproduction in a poverty-stricken country.

Another part of the fertility survey examined what are called intermediate variables. Kingsley Davis and Judith Blake, demographers in the 1950s, reasoned that all people throughout the world go through three steps in reproducing: conception, gestation, and delivery. However, within these three steps are cultural variations, and these variations might affect the number of children who are born into a society and the number who survive. So it was important to compare the patterns of intermediate variables within and between the two towns. For comparing the patterns of conception, gestation, and delivery, the questionnaire had such items as the age when a woman first had sexual intercourse, how frequently she had intercourse, whether she abstained from intercourse for a specified period of time after the baby was born, how long she breastfed, whether she used contraceptives, and whether she aborted or miscarried.

I could not do this survey alone; I knew that I would need a couple of well-trained people to help me. I also knew I needed people whom the women in the town would trust, for the women wouldn't tell such sensitive information to a person with whom they felt uncomfortable or someone they felt was a gossip or a cheat. In Patzún I needed an interviewer who could speak Cakchiquel and who could also read and write Spanish, since that was the language of the questionnaire. I carefully sought the interviewers who would meet the standards—women who were cultural ideals.

Signed with an *X*

After several weeks of talking with various women, I found two ideal interviewers: Felipa Noj and Anna López. Felipa Noj was married with three children and was from a respected family in Patzún; she could read and write Spanish and spoke Cakchiquel, her first language. Anna López was a widow with two small children living in Zaragoza. She worked as a teacher's helper and was well respected in the town.

Training each of these women was fun, since they were eager to learn and also to earn some extra money. I practiced the interview process over and over with them, role-playing all types of women: some difficult, some liars, some ordinary.

I instructed them to get a signed consent form before beginning each interview—a new concept for them. I explained the importance of keeping all information confidential and instructed that if someone didn't want to participate or wanted to quit in the middle of the interview, they were to leave politely. As the majority of women in Patzún were illiterate, we had lots of consent forms signed with *X*'s. Before beginning the actual survey, we pilot-tested the questionnaire. Felipa and Anna practiced their interviews on three families, and I trailed along with them just to see how they did. We discovered that we had to make some changes in the questionnaires.

Felipa Noj, patzuñera cultural ideal, interviewer in household survey

Since Felipa conducted her interviews in Cakchiquel, I asked her to tape-record some of her interviews, so that I could see whether she was adhering to the written Spanish words. I took the tapes to my old friend Magdelena from the Behrhorst Clinic and asked her to write out in Spanish the questions and answers that Felipa had read. This process, called *back-translation*, is tedious, but important when dealing in a nonwritten language. An accurate back-translation means that the interviewer is adhering to the research plan and that the data are valid and can be used to compare with other data. I had Felipa tape-record eight of her interviews (10 percent of the sample) for back-translation. Felipa was an excellent, reliable interviewer. I also went with her to observe five of her interviews; although she was a little nervous with the first observed one, she was very thorough. In Zaragoza, Anna was a fast learner, but her responsibilities as a teacher-helper meant that she wasn't able to do as many interviews a day, and her work lagged behind most of the survey.

I paid two quetzales for every successfully and accurately completed long questionnaire (these took about two hours to complete) and one quetzal for a short questionnaire (which took about a half-hour). These were good wages, considering that the average wage for a male was a quetzal for a day's work and recalling that Señora Caj earned only two quetzales a week for her weavings. Anna completed fifty-seven long questionnaires and twenty-five short ones in Zaragoza; Felipa completed fifty-six long questionnaires and twenty-six short ones in Patzún. This meant that eighty-two questionnaires were completed in each town. How was that number determined? And how were the households identified?

Random Sampling in Towns without Addresses and Telephones

The above questions frame the need to understand random sampling in any population, but especially in a developing country, where the usual methods of sampling have to be modified. The actual number of households used in a random sample depends upon the level of probability a researcher wants his or her findings to have. I wanted to be able to compare the findings so that I could make statistically significant statements with a 95 percent level of confidence. With this level of confidence, these findings could be compared with what is found by other demographers throughout the world. Because of the lack of house numbers and such, I felt that I needed to allow for a 35 percent sampling error, meaning that I would use a sample of a larger number of households than might be used to do a survey in a country such as the United States. Researchers do not want to sample more than is necessary, because surveys are expensive and time-consuming. I had planned to use Cloyd's Tables (see Cloyd, 1973; many others are also available) for determining my sample size, but first I had to determine how many households there were in each town!

I was lucky to find that Guatemala has a fairly sophisticated system of map making. Each town is mapped every ten years, and these maps are for sale in a little-known geographical center in Guatemala City. I would never have known this if I had not had the fortune to meet Gary Elbow, a doctoral student in geography from the University of Texas. He was doing his research in a larger town west of Zaragoza, and we had become acquainted, since he would travel through Zaragoza on his way to his research site. He knew many details that were helpful to me in my research. I went to Guatemala City and found the maps, just as Gary had said. I checked the accuracy of the large maps by walking up and down the streets of each town, checking the descriptions and points of reference. I did not check each house; however, it seemed that only a few changes had occurred in each town, since the maps were made only about five years earlier. There were numbers on a few of the houses in each town, but I felt it would be far more accurate if I numbered the houses indicated on the maps and then drew a random sample from a table of numbers. These random numbers could then be matched with the numbered houses on the map.

So I stretched out the maps on my living-room floor and went about systematically numbering the houses. The work was tedious, but necessary. There were 784 houses in Zaragoza and 1,220 in Patzún. I knew that the houses in Zaragoza were neolocal and would likely have a smaller number of people living in them than those in Patzún, which were compound houses. I wanted to be certain that the sampling process was the same in each town so that the comparisons would be accurate; therefore, I decided to use *household* to mean "a family that cooks together," because within the compound houses, there were natural "households"—usually nuclear families—that cooked together and identified themselves as households. I found that each of these families also identified themselves as one economic unit. For instance, in the compound house in which I lived in Patzún, each of the families, or households, had an identified household income, even though all the people living in the house worked cooperatively.

With the random numbers picked, I marked each sample-house on the map with a red *X*. Within each sample-house, every woman between the ages of fifteen and forty-nine was to be interviewed (provided she granted her permission). If the red *X* fell on a compound household, each household in that compound was to be interviewed. I explained my research plan to several demographers before beginning and gained assurance that the method was accurate.

Is Anybody Home?

Felipa and Anna each had a map and the list of households they were to interview. The maps were divided into quarters, and they were to survey one quarter before moving on to the next. When a sample-house had a number on it, this was written on the questionnaire; if a house didn't have a number on it, the directions were described according to some geographical context or landmark, such as "fourth house to the left and across from the pila in cantón coyote." The interviewers would describe any permanent feature of the house, such as "has shutters on windows," in order to allow any other researcher who wanted to do a restudy to duplicate the original study reliably.

The survey was difficult but necessary. Felipa completed all of the eighty-two interviews in three months. At times she became weary of the process of walking to a remote house (which was difficult, as Patzún is very hilly), not finding someone home, going back, and so on, but I encouraged her with bonuses now and then for her excellent work. People in Patzún wanted to be a part of the survey, so they helped her too. The mayor of Patzún thought it was important to know some of these opinions, and he asked what he could do to help Felipa. I told him, "Just answer any questions from the citizens if they ask you what is going on; this would help." He went one step further and had an article written in the local paper about the study and its importance. This helped us move ahead quickly, and Felipa was encouraged by the interest shown. The mayor was also intrigued with the map, as he had not known it existed. I gave it to him as a gift after completing the survey. When Felipa completed the work, I took her and her family to a local comedor for a celebration—hers and mine.

As I previously mentioned, Anna had more problems, because she didn't have as much time to do the actual interviewing. I thought of replacing her when three months had gone by, because she was less than half-done. I hated to try and train another interviewer, and I hated to hurt her feelings. Some of her questionnaires were done hurriedly and were not as complete as they needed to be, so I withheld pay until she got all of the information. Despite the problems, I knew her data were accurate in the end and that she was honest. I went with her on five of her interviews and found that she was having fun and had quickly developed a good rapport with the women, who were ordinarily a somber group; they were laughing and telling their tales with glee. This experience also gave more depth to my ethnographic fieldwork notes.

Anna also had more problems finding women at home, which surprised me, as I had thought that no woman left her home in Zaragoza! This information caused me to reexamine the women's patterns of activity. Several of the houses had been deserted, but since I had drawn such a large random sample, we had plenty of houses in the sample to meet that magic number of eighty-two interviews in each town. When Anna finally brought the last completed interview to me, she, my mother, and I celebrated with a bottle of *cusha* (the *potent* native liquor). Zaragoza townspeople knew about the survey, but they were not as open about discussing it as were the people in Patzún. This was not surprising, as the Ladinos were more secretive in all that they did. The mayor, however, was delighted to see a map of the town. He seemed to take great pride in the fact that the Republic of Guatemala had thought enough of their little country town to map it. (I didn't have the heart to tell him that all other towns were similarly mapped.) He used that map in several meetings to point out some needed changes in the water supply. I was glad I had gotten it, and I gave it to him when we were finished.

Data Analysis

With the work of doing the survey done, the next step was to analyze the data and to begin to find answers to the riddle. I packed the 164 completed questionnaires into two big boxes, and the children and I drove across Mexico and home to the United States, guarding the surveys with our lives. I spent the next three months sitting at a university computer, using SPSS (Statistical Package for the Social Sciences) to do the statistical calculations. Those were the old days (almost twenty years ago) when the researcher had to enter each number by hand onto large ledgers, using a codebook developed specifically for that research. Then the numbers were punched onto computer cards, validated, and "run" on the big center computers. Many days I would go to the computer center at eight in the morning and not return home until after midnight. The statistics from the survey analysis showed some significant differences, but also many similarities between the fertility rates in the two towns. I could see some meaningful differences in the opinions the women expressed in each town. The intense work that Felipa and Anna had done was paying off. From the cross-tabulations, the multiple-stepwise regressions, and all the descriptive statistics of the women's opinions and values, I knew that I had a greater understanding of how people in Zaragoza and

Patzún planned their families. It would be late in June 1975 when I would again return to Guatemala to do the last phase of fieldwork: putting it all together.

Chapter 17

The Riddle Has Answers

Not even anthropologists or intellectuals, no matter how many
books they have, can find out all our secrets.
—Rigoberta Menchú, *I, Rigoberta Menchú: An Indian Woman
in Guatemala*, 1992

It is foolish and arrogant to believe that even after performing back-
breaking work over a computer or trekking through many cornfields
or genuflecting a thousand times or riding a hundred chicken buses
that all the secrets of Zaragoza and Patzún would be found out. Nor
would the riddle ever be fully solved as to why families continue
to have babies when so many die. Back in the field in 1975, I knew
I understood these people much more than when I first asked this
question in 1971. Comparing the lifestyles in two different towns
showed me their great similarities and differences. The statistical
analyses told me the averages, the modal patterns, of what the
majority did or believed. By analyzing these whole pictures, I found
some answers.

The Mystery of Spacing Pregnancies

The statistical analyses showed that families in both towns had
an average of four children. However, the women in Zaragoza
started to have babies later in life, and then had them closer
together. The reason for this pattern is probably because many
young girls leave Zaragoza when they are about fifteen years old
to work as maids in Guatemala City; then they return, a bit older,

183

to marry someone from the town and to begin their families. Once they begin having babies, they have them at close intervals. In contrast, the Indian women of Patzún have their first babies earlier, beginning at eighteen years of age, but they space them further apart. The final number is the same—an average of four living children. Each household, whether in Zaragoza or Patzún, ultimately assures through childbearing practices that there will be a work force to meet the needs of aging parents (average life expectancy in both towns was forty-four years for women and forty-nine for men). There is a type of social security built into the family structure and into these childbearing practices.

Ladino Families, Extended Families, and Fiestas

Because Ladino families send their children to Guatemala City for cash wages as early as possible, someone needs to do the family farming. The Ladino often rent out their land, but they also have a flexible support system that comes from their complex system of compadrazgo and cofradias. The tightly controlled system is reinforced throughout generations by many fiestas and celebrations of life events (for example, baptisms, celebrations of the fifteenth birthday of females, or funerals). Remember how insistent Victoria was that the Queen of the Corpus Christi—a resident of Los Angeles—would return to Zaragoza, because it was her home? Even though the Ladino families are migratory, they maintain intense bonds, held together through extended, sometimes fictive, family ties.

The Indian family, on the other hand, works as a complex corporate enterprise. They stretch the spacing between births, so that the labor needs of a hoe-and-machete, subsistence farming system can be handled. Multiple family members bring in income from diverse sources: farming, weavings, and market sales. Unlike her Ladino sister, the Indian woman contributes more directly, and perhaps more significantly, to the family household income. I believe this contribution accounts for her greater explicit power in the family structure. The whole fabric of the Indian family is more open and seems more sharing than that of the Ladino family.

In both towns the sexual roles are complementary. In the Ladino town, the Virgin Mary is the cultural ideal and the cult of marianismo is prominent. The life of the Ladino woman is idealized to be one of sacrifice and suffering; it is rewarded with children who care for the mother. She is put on a pedestal by the male and not seen as a sexual object, but, to keep herself on this pedestal, the

Ladino woman has to abide by strict cultural norms, isolating herself behind walls, wearing dark, unattractive dresses, being covered, quiet, and clearly not putting herself in any circumstance that could make her the subject of gossip. She also is protective of her children, as it is through them she retains her rightful property and her power within the family. In this tightly controlled world, the Ladino women help their mates, the migrating men, to uphold their image of being strong, brave, and conquering, as they have to work quite competitively in the wage market in Guatemala City. Male family members not only migrate weekly to Guatemala City, but during harvest times they also work on the coast as well. Their endless migrations are allowable, as the system—with social stigmas and gossip playing major roles—keeps the Ladino wives behind their walls. The Ladino males are expected to satisfy their sexual desires elsewhere than with their pure and holy wives, and this permits some of them to have second wives (discussed earlier) in the City.

In contrast, the Indian world is held together through the cooperation of both men and women. The Indian woman is much freer than the Ladina. She can come and go as she wishes. "My mother" is the cultural ideal of Patzún women, and the characteristics they admire are kindness, generosity, and sharing. The cooperative Indian family is kept intact through shared living quarters and through a patrilocal system as well as a patrilineal inheritance pattern. Working together in the fields or in the market, the Indians share their household income. The patzuñeros live in two religious worlds—Catholicism and folk catholicism. The family ties continue strongly attached, as they retain a modified system of ancestor worship.

Equality of Indian males and females is notable. Women help in the fields as well as bring in money through the sales of their handiwork. The dress worn by men and women further communicates that Patzún is an egalitarian Indian town: the styles are similar and complementary. Even the manner of Indian women speaks to equality; they laugh and walk about openly. The incident where the woman came to the rescue of the drunken man illustrates that women are not afraid to speak up and often do so. Indians walk together as families throughout the highlands; extramarital affairs are not tolerated—they would damage or destroy the tightly dependent family structure.

Cups of Clay

In the beginning . . . God gave to every people a cup, a cup of clay, and from this cup they drank their life (Benedict, 1934:38).

In a very real way, both the patzuñeros and zaragozaños have been given cups of clay. In both towns, the people are poor— opposite sides of the same coin. They are primarily subsistence farmers who earn additional income from sales in the markets or by migrating to Guatemala City for seasonal work. Inhabitants of both towns have to sustain their social systems under severe conditions—such as hurricanes, erupting volcanoes, and political unrest. Keeping the rules is important in both towns, and traditionalism is rewarded, since too much change is a threat to the society. Yet change can be expected, and it is anticipated. The newer voices of the younger generations call for more rights and privileges for both sexes. This mindset is present in the Western wear of the men and in the dreams of the young girls, some who wish never to marry.

The need for education is high on the priority list for both peoples, especially the need to become literate—to read and write Spanish. Religion plays a significant role in both towns by sanctioning the cultural rules (recall the cofradia and compadrazgo systems), and the informal religious system is important to all ages. These structures provide explanations for daily events—such as the deaths of 50 percent of the children before the age of five years and the confiscation of land by more powerful people who force farmers to cultivate less productive land. Think of the two crosses in the remote areas of the Guatemalan highlands and remember the story of the early Maya and their wish to retain their gods. These events were too mysterious and painful for people to comprehend; they needed explanations and found them through their religion. *Diós sabe.* God knows. Even today, as the political suppression continues, the people remain resourceful and resilient.

On My Way Back Home

September 1975 arrived—nearly a year had passed since we began the household survey. It was time for me to finish my fieldwork, and my feelings became mixed. On the one hand, I longed to return home to my big house, warm showers, television, and most of all, my family. The desires to return to the usual—the expected—and to reenter my American lifestyle called to me as a

A cup of clay—each culture has its own way of life

siren song. I felt I had accomplished the goal of beginning to discover
the meaning of variations in lifestyles and how these fit within a
larger cultural context and I was ready to go home. On the other
hand, I had to say farewell to the people and places that had become
so much a part of my life.

In Patzún, I said good-bye to the Maczul family and left my cot
behind with many memories. The family seemed accepting of this
event, as they were of so many others. It just was—a beginning and
an end. There were no tears or ceremonies, only a special weaving
tucked into my bag as a gift of remembrance. I genuflected as I left
Mother Maczul behind at the doorway. I said good-bye to the mayor,
to Padre Sergio and the sisters of the Colégio San Bernardino, to
the children, and to the beauty of the hillside town and took my

last trip along the Ribbon of the Seven Deadly Sins back to Zaragoza.

Saying good-bye in Zaragoza was different, as my house had been a meeting place for many. I was one of the first outsiders who had ever come to be a part of them. The zaragozaños were aware that they were a disliked people, and some felt that I had overcome that curse by *liking* them—and I really did. My feelings were strong for the people in both towns, but they were stronger for the people of Zaragoza, perhaps because it was here that I struggled the most. Or perhaps it was because I could speak and understand their native language, Spanish, and I could never master the language of Cakchiquel beyond a superficial level. That limitation is a difficult barrier to overcome in any research.

The night before I was to leave for the United States, my fictive zaragozaña family had a big fiesta at my house. They began cooking the meal in my backyard days before the party. "I don't trust your gas stove," Silvia explained, "so we will just cook as we always do, over the charcoal."

The smells were delicious, filling the whole street. As the marimba band arrived, they threw pine needles on the ground in my backyard and on the patio. I dressed in a long, formal pink gown and completed my attire with a rhinestone necklace, quite different from my usual white blouse and black skirt. It's time to be festive, I thought, to show your appreciation for their kindness. The night was warm and clear as the music began. People—young, old, men, and women—filled my house from six in the evening until nearly two the next morning. I believe nearly everyone in Zaragoza came at sometime during the evening—teachers, students, the nuns, the mayor and his wife, the councilmen and their wives, my dearest friends. At midnight the liquor was still flowing, but no one became drunk; I believe everyone danced too much to be affected by the drinks. I danced each dance, so I did not touch a drop. By two o'clock the musicians and I were exhausted. I shared my last dance with my four best companions: Victoria, Juan, Anna and Jorge. I cried a bit as we circled around and around. With that final song, the musicians took their instruments and departed and, along with them, my friends.

The night was too short, I thought as I stumbled into bed on my last night in Zaragoza. Morning came the same way it always had: a sudden burst of light and racket, people milling into the street, and the rooster crowing. Then came a knock on the door: it was my good friend and confidant of five years, Dr. Eugénio Schieber, the man who owned the beautiful refuge at Lake Atitlán. He had promised my husband that he would see me safely onto the highway heading toward the United States. He paused for a cup of coffee and the ritual my mother put us through of saying the rosary and pouring holy water over my head and anointing my back. Her prayers were filled with her tears. Within a half-hour I had filled my car with last-minute things and was on the road. The cloud of dust dimmed the view I had of Muñeca, my golden dog, who ran behind my car and somehow seemed to sense that her new home could not be half as generous as mine had been. My eyes filled with tears as I tried to see it all for one last time. As the tires of my car struck the Pan-American Highway, the last of the snowy-white tombs of the Zaragoza cemetery sank behind the mountainside. I was on my way back home.

Twenty years have passed since I first drove into the highland region of Guatemala and began to study it and, eventually, to know its people. My work in Guatemala had become the turning point of my career and became the turning point for other discoveries throughout my professional life. As a result of that time and its teaching, I still become concerned when I learn of family planning programs that focus, too narrowly, on a better condom or contraceptive pill, or on "bombing" places with modern contraceptives— so that people have "access to modern contraceptives"—*without trying to understand the meaning of family procreation within a specific cultural system.* Let's not forget that Baby Rosa died in her mother's arms not for lack of family planning or because she wasn't wanted and wasn't needed. She *was* needed and wanted, as had been her brothers and sisters who preceded her in death. Let's not forget the young boy/man who died of lockjaw just at a time when he would begin to help his aging parents. Let's pause to recall the losses experienced from disasters Fifi and Fuego and wonder how many people went hungry after that winter. Remember Tina's cry. Jorge didn't hear the babies' cries from hunger as she did. Remember that spacing babies makes more sense in different economic systems. Sometimes it's better to have all the children close together, while other times a work force is needed to cover two decades of labor. Don't be hasty, or rush to judgment, but rather sit quietly and observe just how the people are coping using their own patterns of adaptation. Perhaps this ethnography will help you or others in learning the complexities of family reproduction and other social behaviors. I hope it will serve you well in your inquiries into and proposed solutions for life's most demanding, complex, and long-standing human problems, especially as they pertain to societies like Patzún and Zaragoza, where so few options exist.

Chapter 18

An Epilogue
Returning Time and Again

The 1976 Earthquake

I successfully defended my dissertation on January 17, 1976; and only two weeks later, at 3:04 A.M. February 4, the lives of the people of Zaragoza and Patzún were torn apart, as were those of the majority of people in the whole Republic of Guatemala. A massive earthquake, measuring 7.5 on the Richter scale, shattered the tiny adobe homes and cane huts of the two towns, as well as most of the homes in the Department of Chimaltenango and throughout the country. Over 25,000 people were immediately killed and over 75,000 were severely injured. The devastation splintered the country.

An unofficial count of those in Zaragoza who died was 1,000 and in Patzún, 2,000. Mass graves were the final resting places for many. Aftershocks, about 2,000 of them in the next two days, left the people fearful and tense.

I left Colorado as soon as I could, traveling as a volunteer for the Salvation Army. I was flown to Guatemala, free of charge, by Mexicana Airways, and stayed at a local hotel, armed with food and water from the United States. After arriving, I went immediately to the Emergency Headquarters for my assignment. I was incredibly surprised when I learned that the Salvation Army, only one among approximately 100 relief agencies, had been assigned to take emergency supplies to Zaragoza and Patzún! This is unbelievable,

I thought. Of all the possible places to which I could have been assigned in the whole country of Guatemala, I was assigned to "my" villages. The next morning twelve male volunteers and I loaded a large truck and headed into the highlands. The devastation was unbelievable. The road had diminished to crevices, and huge bridges hung in dangling pieces. We crept upward through the hillsides, slowly testing our way. Aftershocks continued throughout the trip. Finally, after sunset, we reached Zaragoza. Although a trail had been cleared, the once-straight streets were now merely a pile of rubble. The only structures left standing were the município, the market, and part of the school. The cathedral across the street from my house had crumbled onto the convent, killing all six of the Guatemalan nuns living there. All of the houses in the town had been leveled. (I recalled how carefully I had numbered each of the houses for the questionnaire in order that the same houses might be located when I or another researcher would do a restudy.) Only the front door and window of my own gringa house stood intact; all the rest was rubble. People were sheltered under cardboard boxes, canvas tarpaulins, or whatever covering they could find to protect them from the cold nights of winter.

As we, the Salvation Army volunteers, handed out food, blankets, and clothing, by the light of a gasoline-run motor, streams of townspeople told me of the horror of the "night of the fourth." Many wept, recounting the number of burials that had to be made. They all said, "We knew you would come." My neighbors came and held me tightly, trying to squeeze some strength from me—one who had not been there, but still cared for them. A next-door neighbor screamed into the night telling me about the death of her three-year-old daughter—the one I used to carry around my patio and who often came to ask me for cookies. Silvia, my mother, believing that I would come to help, came running to give me a drink of cusha. Before leaving Guatemala City, wanting to have my hands free to work, I had filled my bra with quetzales, so that I could give to the most needy. When I left Zaragoza, it was considerably reduced, so I called it my cross-your-heart bra. Why had this disaster occurred? Why this great destruction? Again and again, I heard the same story: a giant serpent wanted to get out of the ground beneath us, and his surfacing had shaken the earth. The people also informed me that the chapel of San Simón, the one I had visited with Maria, was the only building standing for many kilometers around. They told me that many people had seen San Simón, the folk saint of Latin America, the night of the earthquake, asking for alms. They saw his appearance as a sign of the need to repent and to ask for his blessing.

Because the roads between Zaragoza and Patzún had been completely destroyed, I was unable to enter Patzún; however, the accounts were devastating. Rumor was that this town had also been completely destroyed. I did go to the Behrhorst Hospital, where over 5,000 Indians had come to be cared for, not trusting the United States field hospital that had been set up down the road. They came to the place they trusted. I ended this experience with a question: what would happen to Zaragoza and Patzún?

Post-Earthquake Study, 1977 to 1982

After the trip as a Salvation Army volunteer, two other social scientists—Fred Bates of the University of Georgia and Tim Farrell of the Instituto de Nutrición Centro América y Panamá—and I were funded over a million dollars by the National Science Foundation (NSF) to do a longitudinal study of the rehabilitation and recovery of a whole country following a devastating natural disaster. This quasi-experimental study lasted five years and included nineteen research and six control sites. Zaragoza and Patzún were among the research sites (those with heaviest damage), so I returned to these two highland towns week after week for almost five years until we concluded the study. My major focus in this NSF study was the squatter settlements in Guatemala City, and elsewhere I have written extensively about that work.

Most of my closest friends and neighbors in Zaragoza and Patzún had survived. My fictive Zaragoza mother and father, Silvia and Pablo, quickly rebuilt their home and tienda. The zaragozaños continued in their scrappy, competitive style, never agreeing on anything. They even fought over which should be rebuilt first— the cathedral or the school. The cathedral won. The zaragozaños believed that they must repent of their sins and that rebuilding the cathedral was one way to show their repentance. Education would come later, and it took several years before the school was reconstructed.

After the earthquake, the people of Guatemala were bombarded with aid from foreign countries—over 100 countries responded. Each country had adopted a town, and the country to adopt Zaragoza was Spain. The Spanish relief was slow in coming and many problems arose, but finally all the houses were rebuilt, and the water supply was reestablished. The Spaniards did one unusual thing: they built new homes for those who had lived in cane huts on the edge of the town. Remember the Hernández family, the poorest-of-the-poor with whom I had stayed overnight? They received land, plus a two-room, cement-block house. Tina began cooking for one of the builders, and Jorge became a day worker; each received a regular wage, and they began to live a different life. Their children were enrolled in school and progressed well. So much, in their case, for the theory of a culture of poverty!

In Patzún things were different. Because the major road from the Pan-American Highway was never rebuilt properly, it continued to disintegrate, and tourists refused to drive on it. The townspeople lost their income from the weavings and other tourist articles. The Colégio San Bernardino also suffered heavy damage from the earthquake but it was finally rebuilt—even bigger than before—by the country of Colombia. The Colégio San Bernardino continues to be the mecca of education for the Cakchiquel children.

Norway was the country that volunteered to rebuild Patzún. The Norwegians were a very efficient bunch of volunteers and built superb cinder-block homes. The patzuñeros continued in their cooperative style, making a plan and sticking with it. The schools, the cathedral, the churches, and the municipal buildings were all rebuilt in record time. In fact, all of the homes were rebuilt within a year. The style remained the same, but there were fewer compound houses, as each extended family maximized on the opportunity to have its *own* home built. Padre Sergio urged that the magnificent cathedral not be rebuilt, that these funds instead be used for social good, yet in spite of his wishes, three years later the cathedral was reconstructed. These changes were subtle but still perceptible in the town of Indian power.

As the country rebuilt, so did the army. The rebel forces and the regular army fought throughout the highlands. In many ways this violence was a more devastating disaster than the earthquake. People were assassinated or "disappeared" in both Zaragoza and Patzún and throughout the highlands. Almost all of the promotores from the Behrhorst Program were killed. Some villages were left entirely without people—all were assassinated. In others only women and children remained. Terror ruled the land. On my last trip into Zaragoza in 1982, in the final stages of the National Science Foundation research, I visited Silvia, my fictive mother. We had finished eating lunch and were chatting when the door burst open and in marched about forty military men, armed with machine guns. My mother was noticeably shaken—the first time I had ever seen her frightened—but she tried to cover it by offering the men peaches from the trees in the courtyard and sweets from her store. They wanted to know why a tall, blonde woman was in her house. My mother explained that I used to live there and that I was a friend of hers. They looked at my passport and papers suspiciously but finally agreed that I was harmless. Then they left. As soon as the door shut, my mother fell on her knees crying and praying, loudly. She said, "Leave quickly before they come back, and never come back to Zaragoza. You have marked our home as one to be watched." I could not help feeling hurt, but I understood the gravity of the situation and knew that she was right.

"Only send letters," she called to me, as she slammed the door shut. I could hear the locks click behind me. I quickly got into my car and sped back to Guatemala City. Within days I left Guatemala, because it was too difficult to work in the highlands at that time. Most relief agencies had pulled out, and even Doc Behrhorst had to leave for a few months. Since our study was finished, I had no reason to return.

Semana Santa, 1987

New elections had seemingly calmed the country. It was Holy Week of 1987 when my daughter, now twenty-two years old, and I returned. As we entered Zaragoza, I could hardly believe my eyes. It was beautiful! The fountain was working, and the plaza was filled with green grass and flowers. The school had been completed and looked well cared for. The soccer field was in place, and the cathedral looked magnificent. The streets had been paved and new street lights were everywhere. We drove up and down the paved streets (now four) and up the hill where the houses for the poor had been built by the Spaniards. They were still there; some looked neglected, but others seemed to have had more rooms added. The casa de la gringa had been reconstructed and was repainted pink and blue.

During the time that had passed since my post-earthquake study, my fictive mother and father, Silvia and Pablo, had died, of natural causes. Though I heard once or twice a year from their daughters and from others in the town, I saw no one I knew. I went to my old familiar tienda and caught my breath as a young stranger appeared at the counter, not my familiar mother's face. Yes, things had changed.

"I used to live here," I said to the young clerk. "I must say that things look pretty prosperous now, and it seems much prettier in Zaragoza than when I lived here in 1974 and 1975. What has happened? Do you have a good mayor?"

"Oh he's okay, but we now have a chicken factory just outside the town; just about everyone is working there now."

I could hardly believe it as she explained the source of wealth in the town. I dimly recalled talking with my neighbor one day saying, "You women of Zaragoza should start a chicken factory here in Zaragoza, as the town is so close to the road that goes into the capital, and you all know how to raise chickens in your backyards." Who knows if that comment took hold and became a reality? Whatever the reason for the change, it was good to see the prosperity.

Patzún, we found, had not changed that much. It looked very similar—the market, the cathedral, the pila for washing clothes by hand still existed. We found Padre Sergio at San Bernardino looking more frail, but still joyous and active. My American nun companions had left; one was leading a school in Colombia, and the other had returned to the States. The Maczul family was now split, living in several compound houses. They were still growing wheat and corn, much as they had in 1974 and 1975. The eldest daughter, who had married the lesser man, had learned to read and write, and she laughingly told me, "I'm now looking for a younger man." Perhaps it was the beginning of a feminist movement, I mused. I asked about the Caj family, who had lived in the cane hut with the black snake as a rat catcher. No one knew what had happened to them; some couldn't remember that they had ever lived there.

Other Changes

My friend Magdelena Katok became ill and could no longer work at the clinic or in Xajáxac. Edith, the British midwife, returned home and received a special honor from the queen of England. Doc Behrhorst's work continues as he had dreamed it would. Two Cakchiquel men completed their medical degrees and have assumed responsibility for running the hospital, clinic, and program. The program has changed its name from the Behrhorst Program to a new title reflective of Doc's vision, Nuevo Amanecer, meaning the New Dawn. In May 1990, two weeks after the final negotiations for the New Dawn, Doc Behrhorst died of a heart attack. While his work was ended, the program lives on. He was buried with great honor in a peaceful valley near his home in Chimaltenango.

My friend Dr. Eugénio Schieber continues to live at his beautiful home on Lake Atitlán, but he travels worldwide, having become a renowned plant pathologist specializing in avocados.

My life, too, has changed. My husband and I divorced several years ago. I have taken positions at other universities: Illinois, North Carolina-Chapel Hill, and Arizona. I also held a position with the

World Health Organization, working as the Regional Advisor in Nursing, the Western Pacific Region. My children have both become responsible adults and parents.

One thing that hasn't changed is that people still come from all over the world to see the place where dreams are made real— Guatemala—the Land of Eternal Spring. And I know that I, too, will keep returning to the mountain again, and again.

References

Aamodt, Agnes M. 1992. Toward Conceptualizations in Nursing: Harbingers from the Sciences and Humanities. *Journal of Professional Nursing* 8 (May-June): 184–94.

Adams, Richard N. 1964. *Encuesta sobra la cultura de los ladinos en Guatemala*. Publicación no. 2. Guatemala: Seminario de Integración Social.

_____. 1970. *Crucifixion by Power: Essays on Guatemalan National Social Structure, 1944–1966*. Austin: University of Texas Press.

Benedict, Ruth. 1934. Cups of Clay. In *Patterns of Culture*. Boston: Houghton Mifflin.

Bohannan, Paul. 1992. *We, The Alien: An Introduction to Cultural Anthropology*. Prospect Heights, IL: Waveland Press.

Borah, Woodrow Wilson. 1963. The Aboriginal Population of Central Mexico on the Eve of the Spanish Conquest. Vol. 45 of *Ibero Americana*. Berkeley: University of California Press.

Casteneda, Carlos. 1968. *The Teachings of Don Juan*. Berkeley: University of California Press.

Cloyd, Thomas. 1973. Tables for Determination of Proper Sample Size. Mimeograph. Boulder: American Institute of Behavioral Sciences, University of Colorado.

Coe, Michael D. 1966. *The Maya*. New York: Praeger.

Davis, Kingsley, and Judith Blake. 1975. Social Structure and Fertility: An Analytic Framework. *Economic Development and Social Change* 4 (April): 211–35.

Estés, Clarissa Pinkola. 1992. *Women Who Run with the Wolves*. New York: Ballantine.

Gaitán, Hector. 1976. *Vida y Milagros de Maximón*. Guatemala City: Plus Ullra.

Geotz, Delia, and Sifanus G. Morley, eds. 1950. Translated by Adrian Recinos. Popul Vuh: The Sacred Book of the Ancient Quiché Maya. Norman: University of Oklahoma Press.

Giraldo, Octavio. 1972. El Machismo como fenómeno psicocultural. *Revista Latinoaméricana de Psicologia* 6 (3): 295–309.

Glittenberg, JoAnn. 1976. A Comparison of Fertility in Two Highland Guatemalan Towns: A Ladino and an Indian. Ph.D. diss., University of Colorado, Boulder.

Golde, Peggy, ed. 1970. *Women in the Field.* Chicago: Aldine.

Harris, Marvin. 1975. *Cows, Pigs, Wars, and Witches: The Riddles of Cultures.* New York: Vintage.

Humbertson, E. Michael. 1976. *Los Escándalos de Maximón.* Guatemala City: Ministerio de Educación.

Kay, Margarita A. 1982. *The Anthropology of Human Birth.* Philadelphia: F. A. Davis Company.

Lewis, Oscar. 1962. *The Children of Sanchez: An Autobiography of a Mexican Family.* New York: Random House.

Luecke, Richard, ed. 1993. *A New Dawn in Guatemala: Toward a Worldwide Health Vision.* Prospect Heights, IL: Waveland Press.

Mead, Margaret. 1959. Dominant Cultural Attitudes in Manu'a. In *An Anthropologist at Work.* Boston: Houghton Mifflin. (Originally published in 1930 as Social Organization of Manu'a in Bishop Museum Bulletin, No. LXXVI, Honolulu.)

———. 1979. *Some Personal Views.* Edited by Rhoda Metrauz. London: Angus and Robertson.

Menchú, Rigoberta. 1992. *I, Rigoberta Menchú: An Indian Woman in Guatemala.* Edited and with an introduction by Elisabeth Burgos-Debray. Translated by Ann Wright. London: Verso. (Originally published in 1983 as *Me llamo Rigoberta Menchú y así me nacio la concienca.* Barcelona: Argos Vergara.)

Méndez Dominquez, Alfredo. 1967. *Zaragoza: La Estratificación social de una comunidad ladina guatemalteca.* Publicación no. 221. Guatemala City: Seminario de Integración Social Guatemalteca.

Morales Mateo, Urrutia. 1961. La Division politica y administrativa de la República de Guatemala. Book 1. Guatemala: Publicacion, República de Guatemala.

Mörner, Magnus. 1970. *Race and Mixture in the History of Latin America.* Boston: Little, Brown.

Peck, M. Scott. 1978. *The Road Less Traveled.* New York: Touchstone.

Rays, Ralph L., trans. 1933. *Book of Chilam Balam of Chumayel.* Publication no. 484. Washington, D.C.: Carnegie Institution of Washington.

Rosenblat, Angel. 1967. The Population of Hispaniola at the Time of Columbus. *Native Population.* Mexico City: D. F. Mexico.

Simon, Jean-Marie. 1987. *Guatemala: Eternal Spring—Eternal Tyranny.* New York: W. W. Norton.

Tax, Sol. 1953. World View and Social Relations in Guatemala. *American Anthropologist* 54 (January-March): 27–42.

Wolf, Eric. 1959. *Sons of the Shaking Earth*. Chicago: University of Chicago Press.

About the Author

Jody Glittenberg is Professor and Head of the Mental Health Division of the College of Nursing at the University of Arizona. She first visited the Guatemalan highlands in 1971, as a young nurse and graduate student working at the famous Behrhorst Hospital. After completing her doctoral fieldwork in the highlands, she was a Coprincipal Investigator on a National Science Foundation grant for over five years. She has held professorships at the University of Colorado, the University of Illinois at Chicago, and the University of North Carolina at Chapel Hill. She has been the Regional Advisor for Nursing with the World Health Organization in the Western Pacific Region and was a Visiting Scholar at the Lincoln Insitute in Melbourne, Australia, and at the Queensland Institute in Brisbane, Australia.